Driftwood Press

Issue 6.1

Editors

Credits

Independently published by *Driftwood Press*
in the United States of America.

Fonts: Garamond, Cinzel, League Gothic,
& Merriweather.
Cover Image: Alexander Landerman
Cover Design: James McNulty & Sally Franckowiak
Magazine Design: James McNulty

Published in January 2019
ISSN Print: 2578-7195
ISSN Online: 2331-7132
ISBN-13: 978-1-949065-01-5

Please visit our website at www.driftwoodpress.net
or email us at editor@driftwoodpress.net.

Table of

Contents

TERMINAL VELOCITY

CLAIRE AGNES

Our last dinner as a family had been at Pizza Peddler. It was our Saturday night, post-Communion tradition. My mother liked the grilled chicken salad and my dad liked the cowboy burger and Billy King. I liked Billy King too. He always made Hershey's kisses appear underneath our salt shaker and never laughed when I asked for a green balloon sword instead of a pink rose.

Billy King, one man show, had been working Friday and Saturday nights at the Pizza Peddler for nearly a decade. He competed for the attention of children with the flatscreen that hung directly in the dining room's center, where alternating animated princesses lived out their happily ever afters in digital color. He told bad jokes, inflated animals and tiaras with the pump attached to his belt, stuck pens through dollar bills, and made foam balls disappear from his clenched fist and reappear under my father's Diet Coke. He always closed with that.

When my father disappeared, so did Billy King. I mean, not really, he was probably still twisting balloon animals and sticking pens through twenty-dollar-bills while Jeff slid pies in and out of the oven with his great wooden paddle. But we didn't go see him anymore, even on the nights my mother was too tired to cook. She just started bringing home frozen pizzas from the ShopN'Save instead.

~ ~ ~

It was a routine landing. That's what they told us. His parachute had opened normally, billowing upward as he plummeted through the air. He'd come back in afterwards to bullshit with Todd, who was in charge of manning the register and general bitch work, which here meant answering the phone and cleaning the occasional shit out of a skydiving suit. They told us my father had taken a piss, bought a Coke out of the vending machine, and walked out to his truck, parked in the gravel lot behind the building. He'd taken a left down the dirt road back to civilization, which was really the only option anyway. That was around noon, the owner told us. He was chewing jerky and I could smell it.

He showed us the company flight log, the equipment rental records, and the time-stamped soundless frames from the camera above the cash register. He told us that we were lucky, that he'd only just installed the camera a few weeks back after he'd caught Todd reading an old issue of Hustler behind the counter. He led us to the windowless back office, where we watched my father walk out the doors we'd just walked in. My mother paused there, on that final frame, and the silence settled in that skydiving center in the middle of a wasteland. She had known then. Something about the way he'd nodded goodbye to Todd and pushed through the swinging double doors had told her. He was gone.

~ ~ ~

For the first seventy-two hours after my father's disappearance, my mother was a one-woman call center. She dialed, directed, and delegated as if she could bring him back through color-coordinated organization alone. I sat on our reupholstered plaid couch, watching the steady current of solemn-faced adults as they cycled through our small kitchen. They always entered the same way, a soft knock on the door. Doorbells were too crass under the current circumstances. They slid into the foyer casserole-first. The husbands lingered by the staircase, pretending to examine the woodwork or the wainscoting. The wives would infiltrate the kitchen, wrap their arms around my mother, scan the refrigerator door and the countertop for any shred of gossip they could swap for social currency.

I half-listened from the den, a book propped open on my lap, the ceiling fan turning the pages for me. The room had been designed by my mother to be "elegantly understated." My father had wanted to paint it red, but it wound up eggshell anyway. Red might have been nice, though.

I was thirteen when he disappeared, capable of dialing a phone or hanging up posters or talking to the police, but no one asked me and I didn't volunteer. I remembered being six, at the zoo, my father's face close to mine, a wisp of blue cotton candy in his beard.

"If you look up and can't find me in the crowd, don't panic. Just stay right where you are. I'll find you," he said. I had believed him.

My father's leather jacket was still slung over the La-Z Boy recliner. There were dents in the cushion like a memory of him, as if he'd only just gotten up to go get a beer from the kitchen.

Their wedding portrait was on the mantle, framed in silver. The photo was taken in front of St. Mary's Catholic Church, on the steps we took every Saturday. Each of my father's wayward hairs miraculously gelled into submission, even his alarmingly perpendicular cowlick, which no amount of my mother's spit or hairspray could ever seem to defeat in time for Mass. In the photo, their eyes are narrow, mouths open, almost like they were caught mid-laugh. His left arm encircles her, pulling her to him. They are flanked by faces I've never met. The sun slicks their skin and everyone is smiling, but it's my parents who look happiest.

~ ~ ~

The tattoos were the product of a midlife crisis. At least that's what my mother always told people. A few weeks before his forty-fourth birthday, he discarded cattle roping and made himself into a canvas. Every few weeks, he'd tell me we were going to the library, which we always did, eventually, but there was always the stop beforehand, the buzz of a needle, and a massive blue-haired woman with a pair of Ho-Hos tattooed on her right tit. Every time he came home with a new painted patch of skin, my mother locked herself in the bathroom, lit a Marlboro, and called her sister. She would emerge, a few hours later, slip into the kitchen, and the cacophony of cookware would signal that, despite our bad behavior, we would still be getting dinner. He'd wrap his arms around her from behind, kiss her left cheek, and she'd smile. Before they went to bed, she'd take a jar of strong-smelling salve from the medicine cabinet and rub it into his tender, newly dyed skin. Her fingers, coated in that menthol balm, would trace his new tattoo, that night and every night, until the skin had healed.

To my mother, the torso of colored ink served only to attract the cow-eyed stares of bloated housewives at the community pool. They sat, self important and strapped into their one-piece suits, tittering like fattened hens as my father swam laps. To Billy King, they were the beginning of a friendship.

Billy was my father's kind of man, tableside magic notwithstanding. He didn't play golf or wear khakis. He had a condo, an on-again-off-again girlfriend, and no children. He told my parents stories of bartending in Japan and safaris in South Africa, all while twisting a purple balloon into a crown. Tattoos, some bright and some blurred, ran his arms. He had scars on his knuckles and cigarette ash on his jeans. There was a hoop earring in his left lobe, a steel stud in his right.

My mother had insisted that my father limit his new hobby to skin that could be hidden by a polo, so one night, before my father dropped tattooing for target practice, he and Billy left our corner booth to compare ink in the bathroom. My father had just gotten a new back piece, a massive mural that started at his neck and stretched down his spine in black and white. He wanted to show it off.

We could hear them laughing from behind the bathroom door, my father's a thick, unmistakable crack I sometimes still think I hear in a crowd. My mother stared at the bathroom door the whole time they were gone, even though I was stabbing her in the ribs with a Billy King balloon sword.

~ ~ ~

That first night, I sat on the living room couch, about as useful as a throw pillow, well within my mother's line of vision as she jabbed the numbered buttons that would put her in contact with someone, anyone, who had seen her husband.

"Hello," she would say, "This is Jane, David's wife."

She always said it like that, with her voice scaling a note or two higher at the end, almost like she was singing. Even during those desperate calls, with her curls pinned tightly out of her face and that one vein bulging out of the center of her forehead, she had added that slight trill. She was David's wife.

The skydiving center had been one of our first calls, but after she was told that my father had indeed jumped, landed, and left, all with a disappointing normalcy, my mother let their number fall to the bottom of the pile. She hunted for any explanation, save for the one most probable, the explanation shaped in someone else's shadow. After two and a half days of dead ends, however, she had run out of numbers to call and was forced to simply start cycling through the same ones over again, convincing herself that eventually, someone would say that, of course, they had seen him and he would be found sitting at the Montgomery's next door, laughing over a glass of Jim Montgomery's homemade wine.

In the cereal aisle of the ShopN'Save and on the sidelines of soccer practices, neighbors murmured. The hospitals hadn't admitted anyone matching his description. The history on his work computer gave no clues. There was no evidence of foul play.

A few of the Tupperware condolences left on our counters had started to sour in the August sun, so when the man at the skydiving center had told my mother that, if she drove out to their site, he'd stay open and she could watch the security videos and everything for herself, we went.

~ ~ ~

I remember his truck the most. The dust in the radio dial, the stains in the striped upholstery. In the mornings, there would be a mug of coffee in the cup holder. By the afternoon, it would be filled with saliva and chewing tobacco. He used to spit into plastic soda fountain cups, until the summer I mistook the dark liquid inside for a Coke.

I used to feel so special, sitting shotgun, feet up against the dash. He made sure to buy me a granola bar if I was hungry and never seemed agitated when he had to pull over on the side of the road to let me pee. He'd just shield me with his coat or a spare shirt as the cars passed by.

His hobby of having hobbies started with rock climbing, then axe-collecting, followed by bull riding and then archery, flitting from one distraction to the next. Every few months, he'd throw himself into some new activity, mastering some new skill or dead craft. My mother tried to sign him up for the adult baseball league and coordinate golf outings with the other husbands, but the closest my father ever got to a golf club was his two-month stint spent ironworking.

My father, the insurance salesman, would become a fervent addict with every new diversion, filled with an unchecked obsession he let consume him outside the hours of nine to five. But then, just as suddenly as he began, he'd stop. He'd drop whatever it was and never pick it up again, as if he'd never even touched it in the first place. Whenever he could sneak me past my mother, he would take me to his places of diversion, buckled into the passenger seat of his rusted red pickup. If she happened to be home when we left, he'd cobble together some lame excuse, embellished with forehead kisses and a flash of his right dimple. If she was out, he'd scrawl a note on the back of an old receipt, purposefully illegible, and we'd make our getaway before she got back from the grocer. He would bring me into bars without names, into boulder fields and bluegrass festivals, into the basement of a weapons dealer who had a chronically askew toupee, and I would bring a book with frayed binding.

~ ~ ~

The sun was already setting by the time our blue Buick careened into their parking lot. The skydiving center sat at the end of a long, fragmented, red dirt road, which periodically lost itself to the land, like a giant dotted line across the desert. It was built with the sole purpose of shuttling suburban thrill-seekers to the grey, one-story building with its flat roof and the crooked sign out front, which they'd lit up with stadium lights. A handful of small planes rested, scattered on the tarmac until needed on the runway, which streaked darkly away from the building and into the desert's dusk.

I had seen that tiny tarmac only once before, less than three months ago. Jumping out of planes had been just like the rest of my father's hobbies, taken up at random. My mother had spent most of June and July worrying he'd splatter and, by August, he was gone. He had brought me here during those first merciful days of a summer that would eventually shatter the county heat record. He'd only just completed the certification hours required to jump solo, so he ignored the weatherman's windy forecast and woke me while the rest of the world was still dreaming, rocking my shoulder gently so I wouldn't startle and wake my mother.

He held out his bribe with a silent smile – a package of PopTarts wrapped in silver. The real ones too, not the generic kind. The ones with the sprinkles. I wondered how he had managed to sneak such contraband past my mother, but I knew better than to ask him to divulge his secrets. By the time my mother's eyes fluttered open, his truck had slipped the neck of the neighborhood, my knapsack of novels and myself in the passenger seat and the morning sunrise on our tail.

The weatherman had been right, however, and the winds pushed his jump time back farther and farther. He bought me a pack of chips from the vending machine. I drank cooler water out of paper cones. We sat in plastic chairs and after the third delay, I told him I wanted to go home. I told him I didn't understand why anyone would wait around so long just to jump out of a plane and into the sky. He listened with his head half-cocked, his eyes half-averted. We got back in his pickup and drove the two hours home.

He kept going back, freefalling once a week at least, but stopped waking me with a secret smile and a sugary bribe. Those mornings, I'd hear eggs sizzling on cast iron and my mother would be at the stove, a Post-It with his handwriting stuck to the counter.

~ ~ ~

When I was younger, I used to listen to the neighbors fight. I crouched below the kitchen windowsill and listened to what I felt sure were the precursors of divorce. Their jabs were fueled by residual resentments, the resurrected corpses of arguments past. Each spoken spear was engineered to skewer, and I remember feeling grateful for my passive parents, who lobbed insults as incisive as paper-cuts only after they thought I was asleep, hissing like garden snakes so I wouldn't wake.

My father wouldn't just walk away. From her. From me. Even when the owner of the skydiving center read us the exact minutes of the flight log, I couldn't picture it. A numbing denial, instinctual self-preservation I suppose, stopped me from envisioning his landing, light on the waiting earth, bright parachute billowing around him. His steady footsteps leading him away from the landing site, the chute balled under his arm like a beach towel. That was how the August afternoon had transpired. It's all there on the paper.

Yet all I see is my father, plummeting through the atmosphere, ripping a hole in the cotton. The world is bright white streaked with blue and he free-falls through it all. The desert dirt looms below, but he never makes it to the ground. He's falling, falling, falling fast, and then he's gone. He just disappears. Vanishes into air and sky, like he'd slipped through a slit in our atmosphere and fell into another.

~ ~ ~

Two weeks after his disappearance, I sat next to my mother, cross-legged on the tiled bathroom floor. She held a fresh glass of merlot aloft above the lukewarm water as she reclined in the claw-foot bathtub. The tub had been a surprise from my father, an extravagance that my mother had pined for ever since my father took her to see some old black-and-white movie at a drive in, back when they had just started dating. There were a few chips in the porcelain now and I could still see the shadow of the permanent marker I'd scribbled on one of the bronzed feet as a toddler. Now, I couldn't tell if it was the bathwater making the porcelain look dingy, or if it had just slowly greyed as time had inched on by. My mother, lying in the tepid water of her tub, looked tired. I was braiding her hair. A few strands had come loose in the steam. She kept pressing them to her head but, as soon as she brought her hand away, they popped back up, incorrigible.

"The night I met him," she said, "I chose him."

I knew the story. My father was one of a greasy-haired group of guys who smoked pot in the home team dugout that lay hidden in shadows on the farthest corner of the baseball pitch. That particular night was a home game, so my mother was on the adjoining football field, shelling out smiles and high kicks to the packed bleachers, waving her pom-poms as boys collided on the green behind her. Students passed water bottles full of liquor through the crowded rows, chanting with diminishing clarity as the game clock ran out.

In between the baseball and football fields, there was this bare strip of earth that the administration never could get anything to grow on. They gave in the year before I graduated and held this big community potluck, which raised enough for a patch of turf to cover up the bald spot. It always looked odd, just a little brighter and shinier than the grass around it.

But when my mother met my father, that bit of earth was still bare. The game ended and the players, slick with sweat, spilled onto that barren brown soil, followed by their posse of pom-poms, the students with throats rubbed raw by team spirit and cheap vodka, and the fully-costumed mascot—a lion whose hollow shaggy head smelled like cabbage and menthol. They made this huge bonfire right there, in between the fields. Blankets unfurled. The volume of a truck radio got put on high. Someone's older brother came through with beer and cigarettes.

My mother was lost to her memory now, the stem of her wine glass dipping below the water's surface. My knees were numb on the tile. I ran my fingers through her hair and started her braid again.

"He was drawn to the light," she said.

The bonfire pulled the stoners from their dugout cave, but only after the crowd's numbers had shrunk down to a semi-circle of stragglers, clustered around the crackling logs. One of them, the one with jet hair pulled back in an unsecured braid, began softly strumming melodies on an ancient acoustic. The remaining teenagers swayed along to those low, slow songs heard almost exclusively around bonfires. One of the cheerleaders straddled the lion, his enormous head lolling sideways in the dirt. My mother offered the boy with the braid a beer.

"He smelled like chewing tobacco," she said, "and cinnamon."

He had offered her his leather jacket and, even though it was hot in front of the fire, she accepted it and draped it around her shoulders because that's the way these stories always seem to go.

~ ~ ~

Billy King dropped by one Sunday morning. A month after my father's own disappearing act. He didn't bring a casserole, just a six pack. My mother put them in the fridge and made him breakfast because it seemed like the right thing to do.

"Jeff told me why you all haven't been in recently," he said. "How have you been holding up?"

He picked up a piece of bacon with his fingers and dropped it into his mouth. He looked different without the checkered Pizza Peddler tabletop between us.

"We're all as fine as can be," she said, filling the fry pan with soapy water.

When he left, he gave us stilted hugs and said, "Let me know if there's anything I can do to help."

My mother grabbed his wrist.

"If you see him, let me know."

Billy nodded, too forcefully.

"Promise us," she said. "Please."

He looked her in the eyes and said yes. He didn't drop by again.

~ ~ ~

As the frenzy of those first weeks faded, along with the term "missing person," my mother and I slid soundlessly into a quiet coexistence. We passed like ghosts in the halls of our own private mausoleum, remaining in the house that had always seemed too small for the three of us. In St. Mary's and the ShopN'Save, she said, "we're doing well," and smiled with no teeth. When she crossed the house's threshold, she'd slip off her kitten heels, close the door to their bedroom, and I'd soon smell her Marlboros wafting through our empty rooms.

The morning alarm was always followed by the shuffle of her slippers down the hall, then the hiss of the coffee pot and the shriek of the shower handle. The shriek had been my father's legacy, the lone remnant of the bathroom renovation he dove in to, only to quit when the imperfect placement of a grommet made the knob scream and his newborn daughter cry. My mother took her shower without singing, always leaving me enough hot water, and returned to the kitchen, where she applied her lipstick using the reflection in the microwave door as three eggs sizzled on the skillet beside her. She'd look out the window long enough to make sure I got on the school bus, after which she answered phones until three o'clock at the reception desk of a meat shipping company. Wednesday nights were designated for our Neighborhood Association meetings, so every Tuesday evening she'd bake four dozen of something to bring with her. Grocery shopping was done on Fridays, after work, and Saturday evenings were reserved for church.

We diverted like a stream around a boulder, eroding our way around the impasse because we had to. I remember being in high school, taking exams, kissing a boy, kissing a girl, taking a drag from someone's else's cigarette, vomiting peach schnapps into a rosebush, but these memories are all blended and blurred at the edges, like a charcoal sketch you've run your palm over.

~ ~ ~

On prom night, my date had no face. My mother still took photos of us anyway, out in front of the house, hydrangea bushes bleeding perfume all around us. She'd picked out my dress, special ordered from a shop online, dyed periwinkle heels to match. We had spent all morning in the mirror of her vanity. She curled and then teased, pinned and sprayed. She even let me wear her red lipstick, the one she only wore on her birthday. She told me I looked beautiful.

The school gym was buried beneath helium balloon arches and pastel crepe. Girls with AquaNet lacquered curls clung to the elbows of rented tuxedos, delicate corsages already wilting on their wrists. My faceless date evaporated with mentions of punch. I stood in the bathroom line behind ruffled chiffon and wrinkled silk. It didn't matter how beaded the bodice or expensive the fabric, everyone leaned against the taupe tile wall anyway, alternating their weight between already swollen ankles. Lips were glossed, disobedient hairs slicked with water and spit, tampons exchanged, skirts held above hips by generous friends.

I sat on the cold porcelain and spun the empty toilet paper roll in its bracket. A flask passed between French tips underneath the stalls. Someone was crying. Someone was vomiting. Someone was telling a secret. I took the house key from my silver purse, my mother's, borrowed for the night. Its teeth bit the green plastic of the stall, down through the paint into the beige flesh beneath. Each cut made a noise like something begging.

The parachute wound up lumpy, engraved two-dimensional slope not pressed smooth by the influx of air, the rush towards gravity. Its tethers stretched down the paint, arms reaching for the stick figure who should have been attached to their ends. My fingers hurt. I put the key back in my bag and pantomimed washing my hands in the sink.

I found the punch on my own. It was too red and too sweet, spiked so strongly I wondered if one of the teachers tipped the bottle in themselves. I took another sip because it was something to do with my hands, mouth small like with the chalice of Communion wine.

The gym breathed dark and pulsing. A pile of discarded heels sprawled by the door, stiletto tips browned by the photos in family yards and the floormats of boyfriends' trucks. Ties were knotted around heads, vests unbuttoned. The tape had failed one strand of balloons, its purple end dangling like a challenge above the dance floor. This was why everyone took pictures in the beginning.

Two tongues grappled behind the bleachers but I stood there anyway. They wanted to be close to each other and I wanted to be close to them. They didn't seem to mind or notice.

The dance floor felt like a gyrating collection of time. All those hours spent in front of well-lit mirrors, the trips to the malls and boutiques and florists, the matching lipsticks and the delicate rhinestone barrettes and the inhale as the zipper up the back slid shut. Each girl polished into something precious so sweaty hands could hold them, the promise of a night she'll never forget behind each forgone lunch and plucked eyebrow.

I wondered if I had stayed out long enough to make my mother happy. A punch-speckled shirt grabbed a satin breast and I decided I had.

Outside of the gymnasium, Billy King stood, smoking a cigarette.

"Holy shit. You look just like your mom did back in high school!"

I'd seen enough my mother's teenage photos to know he was lying, but thanked him because the comparison was a compliment regardless. I leaned against the brick, arms crossed over my chest, like I'd seen the popular kids do after school.

"You cheating on your Pizza Peddler gig?"

He grinned with all of his top teeth, almost as if he'd really found me funny. He inhaled. The end of the cigarette bled suddenly bright, like a bullseye.

"Kids don't care about magic tricks when they've got phones in front of their faces. They're all such little shits now. Google your trick right in front of you to see how it's done."

I swallowed, mind crawling through a sludge of red punch, grasping for brilliance and settling for sarcasm. I wanted to see his teeth again.

"You mean you aren't really a wizard?"

Billy laughed, exhaling smoke through his nostrils. He held the cigarette out to me. It felt sophisticated between my fingers, so slim and light in its poison. He watched me put it to my lips.

"I'm doing a quick set while the DJ takes a break," he said. "You think these guys are gonna be a good audience?"

He pushed up his black shirtsleeves. A naked woman with serpent hair knelt on his forearm. Her eyes were blank. I took another drag, pausing to make my answer seem important.

"Normally I'd say no, but half of them are drunk already, so maybe you'll have some luck."

He nodded, not at me, but at the cars in the lot, dead headlights looking out from behind cloudy glass.

"What are you doing out here? Won't your date be looking for you?" he said.

The bass of an unfamiliar song beat the brick at our backs. My designated date was somewhere inside. Maybe he had finally found me that punch. Maybe he had found someone else entirely, and maybe they were rubbing non-faces and promising to keep in touch over the summer.

"Can we get out of here?" I said. The words fell from my mouth like they were made of iron, hitting the concrete with a clang loud enough to mute the pounding from the DJ booth. "I mean, can we just go sit in your car for a minute? These heels are killing me."

He snuffed the cigarette's last tendrils of smoke beneath his boot and took off towards a dented black Camaro. The tops of the wheels were rusted and stuffing was spilling from a slash in the backseat. He offered me another cigarette, a whole one to myself this time, hoping smoke might fill the silence.

"How's your mom been doing? Haven't seen either of you in awhile."

"Yeah. We go to Coluccio's now, over on Maple."

A tiny hill of ash fell onto my skirt. I tried to wipe it away and only smeared it to the satin. My mother might think I'd made friends.

"She's a real nice lady, your mom. Better be taking good care of her."

He was looking at the halogen light over the gym door. His jaw was square, like a fact, his chest beneath the black shirt broad, like permanence. He wore hoop earrings in his ears and grew dark stubble along his chin and I imagined what he must have looked like behind that Pizza Peddler bathroom door, shirt lost and tattoos stark under the fluorescent light.

"Did you love my father?"

"We all did."

I don't know who's included in his version of we, if he means himself and my mother and me or if he's talking about a we my father never shared. I wonder how many versions of my father walk the world, how many chapters had been torn out of my copy.

Then Billy was looking at me, wide body turned awkwardly inward, one hand, knuckles haired, on the dash. The way serious adults sit when they have something important to say. I looked at him right back, searching the pores on his nose and the plateaus of his eyebrow for my father's missing pages. His mouth opened and I could see words filled the space behind his canines, inky black and knotted, tangled like steel wool in his throat. They crawled towards the light, staining the air between us grey.

I kissed him. I kissed him quickly. I kissed him hard. My lips were a furtive kick under a table, a knot of hair corked in a pipe, a man in orange on a roadside redirecting traffic around a crash. He tasted tired but his lips moved beneath mine, softening. I put my hand on the thigh of his jeans. He exhaled.

I opened my eyes, just for a second, but it was the wrong second—the same second he opened his too—and then we were suddenly too much ourselves to be so close, our eyes too different, our mouths too sad. It was like looking at the gym after prom night had ended, streamers tattered, balloons sunken, a forgotten purse, a press-on nail.

When I got home, my mother sat at the kitchen table wearing one of my father's old t-shirts and nothing else. It fell to mid-thigh, the normally hidden upper leg somehow more bone bright than the cotton. She made mint tea with honey and swore she could get the ash out of my skirt with a little vinegar. Her fingers freed my hair from the bobby pins and she brushed it slow and humming, like she used to when I was small.

"Did you have fun?" she asked, her voice like a ghost's behind me.

"Yeah," I said. "Did you? At yours?"

The brush fell sluggish.

"Sorry, I didn't mean to—"

"No, no, it's okay," she said. "I had fun. Me and your father, we—"

"You don't have to."

I didn't tell her I couldn't take the hurt it would cost to hear. But she heard it anyway. She didn't say anything else, just pulled a pint of Rocky Road from the freezer and stabbed two spoons into the chocolate.

We slept side by side that night. Not in her bedroom, the possibility she might wake up and mistake my warmth for my father's too cruel a possibility to tempt. We curled beneath my midnight blue comforter and she pointed at a glow-in-the-dark star stuck where the molding met the ceiling, the lone survivor of his former constellation.

"Remember the summer you put those up?"

"I tried to hide them from you guys so hard."

"I always thought they were pretty."

"That's not what you said then."

"Well, you know," she says. "Adults have to say the adult thing."

The ceiling stars, the wide-eyed Furbies, the meticulously cut paper dolls, the gold-embossed volumes of illustrated fairy tales—all victims lost to a mid-middle school room renovation and personality reinvention. There were boxes in the basement, things my mother thought to keep, each cardboard face labeled neatly. My name. A year. A few notes on the contents. Every so often I went down there, even though there's no light until the bottom and you had to walk down the shadowed stairs without exhaling, feeling for the cord my father knotted to the bare bulb's switch. I counted each box, whispered each year into the cobwebs. Six versions of myself lived inside my mother's basement.

She hadn't put my father away, not yet. She might donate his things or sell what she could or burn everything in our front yard or throw each piece of him from her car window on the interstate. But the frame of his John Lennon autograph on the third shelf of the bookcase never gathered dust and so I knew one day his boxes would stack themselves with mine. I wondered what parts of him she'd pack with others. If when I went to college, she might put on one of my father's records and daub her upper lip with the whiskey he kept behind the television and come down to this basement in the darkness to be with her family.

~ ~ ~

My mother started dating Billy King during my last months of high school. She didn't tell me about it. I just walked into our kitchen one day after school to find him halfway through a turkey sandwich and my mother eating orange slices by his side. He sat in my father's seat, at the head of the table. My mother wore lipstick. Her elbows were on the table, chin held up by a soft fist.

He said, "Hey there! How was school?"

My mother smiled at me and it was all she had to say.

"School was great, thanks. How's that sandwich?"

~ ~ ~

On the day I leave for college, my parents' wedding photo watches me go. I feel its stare from the mantle, through the front window, across the cropped lawn, and it makes my feet heavy. Billy loads my suitcase into the back of his Camaro.

My mother's cheek is damp when I pull away. We stare at air beyond our bodies, memorizing blades of grass to keep from breaking. I breathe through my nose to keep my jaw from shaking. My nails excise red sliver moons from my palms until she takes my hands in her own. Her palms are hot and slick. Our eyes settle for patches of one another's faces. A cheekbone or an arch of an eyebrow is all either of us can manage. She asks me questions, the kind all mothers ask their daughters when they leave.

"You'll call when you get there?"

I nod at her shoes, pointed toes wet with morning dew.

"And when you meet your roommate?"

Another nod, this one to the freckle on her chin.

"And when your classes start?"

I squeeze her fingers and bring them to my chest, a few inches of blood and bone between her touch and the tremors in my heart. I imagine she can reach inside me, hold my heart against her breast and trace red circles with her fingertips until it steadies. She doesn't make me promise, not since my father left and took the meaning of the word with him.

She just says, "It's going to be hard here without you," instead.

Her voice is little, like she's afraid of overhearing her own words. Billy slips an arm around her waist.

"I'll be sure you don't get lonely," he says. He kisses her forehead, lips right on the border of her hairline, right where my father's used to rest after the days he plucked me from my bed while she was sleeping.

She holds me close once more, inhales my hair, frames my face with her hands like she is trying to read my future in the reflections flickering on my pupils. We say "I love you" back and forth at least a half-dozen times.

Billy says, "C'mon, you're going to be late for work," and everyone is grateful.

She straightens her blazer and I say, "Have a good day at work," like this is just another morning. We watch her turn out of the drive first, because it's easier. For her or for me, I am not sure.

Billy says, "Ready?"

I sit in his passenger seat for the second time. I buckle my seatbelt, look straight out the front windshield, and turn the radio dial during the Viagra commercials. He doesn't offer me a cigarette today, but at the first intersection, once my mother's house is gone from sight, he starts talking.

"Excited for college? Big step," he says.

The Pizza Peddler shopping center grows and shrinks outside the window.

"I think. It's scary. I don't know who to be there."

"Just be yourself."

He sounds like a motivational poster in a guidance counselor's office. One with a gecko in a bow tie. I nod like he's been helpful. A silver Honda is parked at a tilt on the roadside, a white plastic bag shut in the driver's side, billowing bulbous in the wind.

"Listen, I think we should just clear the air," he says at a whisper, like my mother might hear us through the AC vents.

"No. It's been so long—it's alright."

"It's not. I should've never—I crossed a line."

The words fly from his mouth in fragments, stray syllables ripped from a hundred different imagined versions of this conversation. I watch a bug flatten on our windshield, wings the only part left whole.

"I was the one who—I kissed you."

Billy's back is straight and his hands lock on the wheel, bloodless knuckles pinned to ten and two like mine the morning I tested for my license.

"You were a kid," he says. "Still are. I'm the adult."

I press the ridges of my mother's house key into my thumb. I felt it suddenly, lying cold and flat between my palm and thigh when we pulled onto the highway. I don't remember when I slipped it from my pocket, held it to my skin.

"Yeah, Billy," I say. "But sometimes adults can't act like it. Things make it too hard for them."

The radio switches over to a song my father knew on the banjo. Billy's chest sinks a little — from the lyrics or the chords or a memory, I can't tell which.

"I love your mom. I really do. I don't want—"

I study the mark her key made down my thumb, a seam of red bisecting the skin.

"My mother is happy." I say this because it's true. "Everything is alright." I say this because I want it to be.

His eyes stay wide on the road and I know he is not finished, his real motive the answer to a quiet question.

"You're not going to tell her?" he says, guilt wilting his voice.

I turn to him because I know it's what will make him most nervous, nervous enough to avoid looking back. He sucks the inside of his bottom lip instead.

"You're not going to disappear?"

Our questions straddle one another's chests. The answers are irrelevant. We may even mean them at the time, but nothing promised in Billy King's old black Camaro can keep a man from leaving, a girl from speaking.

"I love her," he says finally, like it's evidence of something.

"A lot of people love her—have loved her."

In the moment, they all mean it. But a memory of someone's words is a lie. It's selfish really, what we're doing. We'll make these pacts to each other and sleep better at night for it, both thinking we've protected my mother, when all we've really done is say what the other wants to hear.

He says, "I know what she's been through."

He says, "I'm not going anywhere."

He says, "I swear."

I wonder if a swear is better than a promise, or if a swear is something people offer only after they've made so many promises the word curdles like a curse. A red pickup truck passes us on the left.

I say, "Can we make a stop?"

~ ~ ~

The squat grey building sticks out like a faded mole in the middle of that wasteland. Two tiny planes border the tarmac. Billy waits in the car, indefinitely.

Among the clouds, the earth is a memory. The plane's twin engines drown out thought, strangle fear, quiet everything that churns inside. The instructor counts down from five. His body folds over mine and I am small once more, like a child who fell asleep in Mass, lifted from the pew to the parking lot by her father's arms.

I plummet through the atmosphere, ripping a hole in the cotton. I see my father. He is falling. The world is bright white streaked with blue and we freefall through it all. The desert dirt looms below, but we never make it to the ground.

Commonalities of Movement and Tone

A Conversation with Claire Agnes

Terminal velocity is the term for the maximum speed an object, or person, falling through the air can achieve—and if a skydiver doesn't pull the ripcord on his parachute in time, the velocity can be terminal in another sense too. In this powerful and moving story, the narrator's father reaches terminal velocity while skydiving, then later that day disappears, terminating his relationship with his family. In the free fall of her grief, his daughter reaches a kind of terminal velocity too, and the girl she was disappears, never to return. Reader, be forewarned: your heart is going to free-fall.

-David Jauss

The following conversation was conducted by managing fiction editor James McNulty.

JM: Congrats on winning the contest, Claire, and thanks for agreeing to speak with me about "Terminal Velocity."

CA: Thank you so much for your consideration of this piece. I am so excited that it's found a home at *Driftwood Press*.

JM: I'd like to open with a question about the emotional authenticity of "Terminal Velocity." There's a sort of emotional rawness to this story that feels so very intimate, and I wonder what goes into crafting that feeling. How much of this work draws on personal experience, and how much of it is entirely manufactured? Could you talk about the elements of "Terminal Velocity" that are autobiographical, if any?

CA: I am the daughter of a blacksmith and a veterinarian, two strong individuals who have shaped my writing and my soul in immeasurable ways. They raised my sisters and I on a small farm and we spent summers camping, hiking, and kayaking. I often joke that my father is the "Liam Neeson of Renaissance Men." He gave me a gift when I was very young, when I was just beginning to fall in love with storytelling. He has always had this hobby of having hobbies, much like the father in "Terminal Velocity," and always took me with him when he could. We didn't have many babysitters or afternoons in daycare and, because of this, I was able to experience the worlds that have now found their way into my creative work.

Writing has always been a process of catharsis for me, a reckoning of experiences, a wrangling of moments into meaning. Each story has some foothold in reality, whether it be through character, place, detail, or tone. Plot is what happens when I am able to synthesize these lived experiences and create something narratively sound.

JM: Much of the story is made up of recollections of the narrator's time spent with her father; this story seems more backstory-heavy than most, yet it never comes off as saccharine. Do you have any advice for other writers who are seeking to emulate this emotional rawness without coming off as unduly sentimental? Did you ever have a tough time tempering the recollections?

CA: The first draft will, almost always, be cringingly sentimental, especially when writing an emotion-driven narrative. I don't think writers should shy away from that. I advocate bleeding onto the page, letting it all out while those portals are still open. Second and third drafts are for trimming, for scaling back, but it is much more difficult to infuse a piece with emotion later, when the starting foundation is apathetic.

My first drafts generally wind up looking like a patchwork of memories, fragments of character and tension that culminate to a certain moment. The second draft is when the knife is unsheathed, where the real structure starts to crystallize. Even if most recollections will not make the proverbial cut, the process of putting them to the page helps isolate the narrative heartbeat.

This being said, nostalgia can weaken recollection-driven narratives. The writing of recollections should attempt to contain itself to the finite tension of the remembered moment without blurring the specific, messy details that make those memories come alive. Speak with truth and precision; take off those rose-colored glasses.

JM: I've often heard that there are two types of writers: those that underwrite and those that overwrite. If that's true, it sounds like you're the latter. Your story seemed to have already gone through several rounds of polish before it entered our submission inbox. Working on it with you was one of the more minimal edits I've done for a *Driftwood* story; much of it came down to fleshing out a few of the final scenes. Could you talk a little about the origins of the story and the long path it took to where it is now?

CA: The writing of this story began with the end. I had an idea for a single scene, a scene that is actually no longer a part of this narrative. However, that direction, that movement towards a moment, that intimate knowledge of the story's emotional core, gave bones to the plot itself. Eventually, the story became strong enough to stand and live on its own. Separating the narrative from that final scene was one of the more difficult decisions I've made while revising a piece, but that fissure allowed for the growth of the work. Now, that scene starts an entirely different story, so it too has found a home.

JM: What happened in the scene you cut, and why'd you decide the story was better off without it?

CA: This story originally covered a much more significant stretch of time, following the narrator into adulthood. It transitioned into a far darker tone and culminated into a graphic sexual scene. The ending was performing similar thematic and emotional work, but it just wasn't the right final note for this story. Ultimately, the juxtaposition between tones became too much weight for the narrative to carry without compromising its integrity.

After workshopping this piece with Joyce Carol Oates, it became clear that this story could go in either direction, but needed to be pushed fully into one tonal realm or the other. I wrote two fresh versions and the truth made itself evident on the page. Once the story was unencumbered by the weight of that final scene, it bloomed in new and dynamic ways. Billy's character was a result of this separation as well, and now it's hard to imagine the story without him.

JM: Is "Terminal Velocity" in any way categorical of your work? You mentioned earlier how you forefront emotion and voice in your writing; does that often lead to intense situations and premises? I'm thinking of the disappearance of our narrator's father as well as the graphic sex scene you've mentioned. It sounds like both of these stories focus around a defining incident and examine the effects.

CA: While the emotionality of the pieces can be intense, I do feel that the bulk of this collection, at least in scene and overt action, exists in the realm of subtlety. This story introduces many thematics that are further explored in other stories, like the intersections of grief and sexuality, queer existence in rural or small town settings, and the influence of formative experiences on female identity.

JM: How far are you into the collection? If all the stories are this good, I'm sure you won't be shopping it around for long. You say this story "introduces" the themes; does that mean the collection opens with "Terminal Velocity"?

CA: This story introduced these themes to me and was the first story in this collection put to page, but I am still playing around with the overall structure. The collection is finally getting to the stage in which I know it intimately, but there are still a couple of stories that need to become more body than bones.

JM: I want to probe a little more into how you use time in your story. For most works of fiction, large amounts of backstory slow down the momentum of the frontstory, resulting in, among other things, a sluggish plot. I suspect this structure works for "Terminal Velocity" because of the balance: you give the backstory equal time and attention. It becomes just as important and riveting as the front story, so we don't mind moving back and forth between them; both the front and the backstory have momentum. What do you make of this structure you've employed? You mentioned your process of writing involves a sort of patchwork inception; does this process often result in similarly structured stories?

CA: Absolutely. Without fail, the bulk of second draft revision revolves around achieving that proper balance. I send first drafts to my readers knowing that the equilibrium between backstory and momentum needs retooling, but like to allow these first attempts to exist, at least momentarily, in the shape in which they've spilled out without muddying the emotional core with concerns of structure. I often find that the opening five pages of any given first draft are where the story searches for its footing. During revision, these pages are usually cut up, sometimes worked into the narrative in new ways and sometimes left in an ever-growing "Scrap Pile" folder on my hard drive.

It is important to note that the "balance" between backstory and frontstory I am referring to is not a compromise. The excitement and viscerality of the frontstory should not be compensating for the anemia and flatness of backstory. To your reader, present action should not be a payoff; recollections should not be penance. Avoid thinking of backstory simply as information that readers need to understand the complexity of the present moment. Passages of backstory are only afforded the same life and vibrancy as present action if the author treats them with equal attention, specificity, and nuance. While I started the process of writing this particular story with the end, this is not the norm. It's often the writing of "backstory" that indicates to me where the story needs to go.

JM: That sounds to me exactly the right way to tackle backstory—using specificity, more detailed flashback than hazy remembrance. All of our editors were quick to note the move to present tense at the end of the story. Though writers such as William Gass, Philip Pullman, and even our guest judge David Jauss have written essays against the misuse and overuse of present tense in contemporary fiction, I suspect many of these writers would concede that it was well-utilized in "Terminal Velocity." Could you talk a little about your decision to switch to present tense, as well as how you feel about the surge of usage in contemporary fiction?

CA: Generally, my stories tend to gravitate towards a particular tense or point-of-view from their conception onward. That being said, I do find it very useful to write accompanying drafts of stories, either in different tenses or from differing points-of-view. This can add texture to the work and open up scenes and characters in fresh, new ways.

This story always contained a shift to the present tense, even in its earliest iterations. It felt like an organic move for this narrator, tone, and scene—a move I hope creates added thematic resonance, but all of these considerations are fundamental when deciding to employ a shift like this so late in the narrative.

To your point regarding the rise of present tense usage in contemporary fiction, this is something I too have noticed, both in published fiction and in the work of my students and peers. I've spent a fair amount of time studying and researching cultural shifts in the language of mass media in an academic setting, with a focus on rhetoric and storytelling structures post-internet. This gravitation towards present tense may be another intriguing side effect of technological advancements in literary culture and tastes. The ubiquity of the internet has put finite pressure and focus on the curation of identity, which has led to a generational desire for authenticity, particularly in storytelling. The popularity of memoir and autofiction has surged, indicating a thirst for truth in narrative. When stories, particularly works of fiction, are written in past tense, that retrospective can put an implied distance between reader and work. This filter can deflate the sense of immediacy, the intimate sensation of a fleeting moment.

JM: I'm not sure I'd agree that past tense puts distance between the reader and the work; for instance, I feel more intimate with the past tense sections in "Terminal Velocity" than I do with the final present tense scenes, though that's probably due more to the tone and narration than the tense. I also suspect many of the authors who wrote all of our classics in past tense would disagree that it lacks immediacy; there are quite many classics that feel far more immediate than present tense contemporary works, so I'm not so sure the forced immediacy thesis rings true. But I understand and frequently see many contemporary writers taking exactly that stance on present tense's "immediacy" when they champion it.

Present tense works so well in "Terminal Velocity" because some of the themes of the work have to do with looking backward, and therefore the switch to present tense at the end suggests more of a forward gaze. How does immediacy play into the ending of your work?

CA: I absolutely agree that past tense has the ability to be just as immediate as present tense on a craft level, if not more so. I'm thinking more specifically about contemporary audiences and why they might prefer narratives rendered in present tense. When considering the curated identities proliferated by the internet and the resulting societal disillusionment, it is possible that readers are put off by past tense because it implies a filter, a retrospective in either structure or character that is counter to this search for true authenticity. This filter is very purposeful in "Terminal Velocity." The shift to the present at the end should function as the loss of innocence, the gaining of sight. The reader should feel something fall away as the narrator herself falls through the sky. If this story started and ended in the retrospective, I fear it would lose its grip on its emotional intensity—that hot, dense core at the center of this story. This juxtaposition of tenses hopes to elicit the emotions tied to each narrative movement while acting in conversation with the story's underlying thematics.

JM: One of our fiction editors, Dan Leach, sent over a good question: "An adult narrator recalling traumatic childhood events has been called one of the trickier balancing acts in literary fiction. Tell us about some of the challenges related to this, especially that of blending adult insight with childlike ambiguities, something you do so masterfully here."

CA: Knowing either my protagonist or plot too well before putting that first draft to page poses a significant hurdle to my writing process. I'm sure other writers work differently, but I've found that being too confident in my knowledge of the narrative or its structure doesn't give the work due breathing room. Full authorial knowledge denies the story its opportunity to surprise the writer or, in turn, her readers.

One of my assets in balancing this narrator's vacillation of childhood and adulthood was the story's emotional core, the voice from which I wrote this story. This protagonist started off with a certain detached numbness, but revealed her vulnerabilities and pressure points to me as the story unfolded. I did not know her fully from the start. If I had, it might have been too tempting to imbue her with certain stale ideals of girlhood and coming of age; however, her ability to surprise me drove the narrative and thematic arcs. Sentimentality can also pose a significant barrier to those writing trauma narratives in the retrospective. It's something I've had to wean out of this story over several drafts, but I believe its initial inclusion benefited the vulnerability of the story overall.

JM: Though I'm generally an advocate for outlining, I agree with the possible pitfall you mention: locking yourself in and therefore stunting discovery. For most writers, there seems to be a sweet spot of mental *preparation* and discovery—where they know something about the protagonist and general direction they want to go before they start drafting, but they only begin to pin it down during that first draft. It sounds like that's similar to your process as well.

There's one ingenious craft moment in this story where the prose alternates between a mother telling a story, through dialogue, in the frontstory and a vividly painted backstory of what she's telling. How much do you think about craft decisions and techniques like these as you draft your initial drafts?

CA: As I was writing that scene, I knew it was going to be difficult to pull off. While there have been minor tweaks to the structure of that moment, it's one of the scenes that has remained the most consistent throughout each stage of revision. I do admit that most of my work sources memory to create emotion, but the linkage of memory to present action is what helps those memories transcend mere "background information" to become something critical to the plot and momentum.

JM: Great. I think we've well covered the how and why of backstory in "Terminal Velocity." Which aspect of the story was conceived first, and which part was hardest to write?

CA: There was an image caught in the webs of my mind, one of my father skydiving, just falling through the clouds. He used to skydive when I was young, but I'm not sure why this visual burned with such lingering intensity. The father's character in "Terminal Velocity" was the first conceived, but he remained floating in blank space until the voice fell into my head. When she arrived, I knew how the two souls would inform one another.

The ending, however. This was one of the most difficult plot movements I've ever had to work through. At one point, I put the story away for a year, its ending open and unfinished, threads left loose and frayed. I felt the work and I were at a permanent impasse, but this story was relentless, slipping into my thoughts even though I hadn't put eyes on its lines in months. It wormed its way into my consciousness, like a weed determined to grow despite the dark. It offered endings and possibilities like samples at a Macy's counter—each distinct, some laughable, some intriguing, but none worth the purchase. Then one day, on an M train back to Brooklyn, Billy King came to me, the ending hoisted over his shoulders. A writer's passion for solving a story's puzzle keeps the narratives percolating, even when we try to distance ourselves.

JM: Quote a piece of writing advice you actively disregard in your process.

CA: Well, of course there's that classic Hemingway maxim, "Write drunk, edit sober," which I have never found to be very conducive to lucid prose. If anything, revision is the time to crack open a beer. But on a more serious note, as a younger writer, I struggled to see myself in much of fiction I was taught in academic settings. The stories discussed in craft lessons were largely all written by straight, white, male authors, our classrooms driven by Carver and Hemingway. A certain type of story was lauded as literary, a firm emphasis on narrative arc and structure, certain types of prose and protagonists. I had difficulty writing about the subjects, contexts, and thematics that fed my passion to write because they seemed to have no place in literature.

My final year of college, I was taught by William Lychack, who not only assigned pieces written by women, people of color, and non-Western writers, but who validated the voices of underrepresented writers within the classroom. I was finally surrounded by stories that resonated, stories that explored lives familiar, stories whose notes hit my soul and echoed throughout my own creative work. I learned that the world of literary fiction was much larger and more dynamic than I had previously realized. Of course, knowledge of the canon of great works and appreciation for their craft is imperative for any young writer, but I would urge those who do not feel intensity towards the works they are studying to seek out authors whose voices may better illuminate their own.

JM: You mentioned Joyce Carol Oates helped this story along in workshop by helping you decide what the tone of the story should be. Did she help in other ways? What other writers have influenced "Terminal Velocity" specifically?

CA: I have workshopped this story with William Lychack, NoViolet Bulawayo, and Joyce Carol Oates, all of whom offered critical feedback on the work. This story has gone through quite a few iterations, so it was interesting to see how each author's reading of the work progressed as the story found its footing. Bill dug into the story's emotive core. NoViolet highlighted the efficacy of voice. Joyce assisted with final structure and tone. I was also very inspired by John Freeman during my graduate program. He reaffirmed my belief in the importance of this story's emotive qualities, the strength of voice. It is always such a gift to see a story transform under the guidance of such incredible writers and individuals.

JM: How about writers you've read but haven't worked with? Which writers and novels have had the biggest impact on your own writing?

CA: My bookshelf priority at the moment goes to Annie Dillard, Maggie Nelson, Denis Johnson, Mohsin Hamid, Edouard Louis, Carmen Maria Machado, Eileen Myles, Alice Munro, Annie Proulx, Laurie Weeks, Melissa Febos, and Charles Baxter. These authors have each influenced facets of my craft, from character to language to setting to voice to magic. While their styles and subjects range wildly, they have each claimed a shard of my soul. I frequently look to their work for craft inspiration, but more often, I open their pages just to bask in the beauty, depth, darkness, and magic of their worlds.

JM: Is there anything else you'd like to tell us about this work in particular as we wrap up?

CA: I am so excited to see this story in the pages of *Driftwood* and want to thank you again for your support of this piece. This manuscript has been clutched so close for such a long time; it's incredibly exhilarating to see it finally take flight in this gorgeous new issue.

JM: Well, it was great delving into these topics with you, Claire. Good luck with your collection; I'll be looking for it on bookshelves soon!

CA: I better get back to my typewriter then! Thanks so much.

Her Noble Face

SHANE PAGE

Palooka pressed his cane into a notch in the sidewalk while he waited for his dog, Silver, to finish pissing. He wrapped the husky's leash around his fingers so she wouldn't wander too far, but Silver always picked the same spot: an alleyway between a deli and a flea market, behind two aluminum trash cans, in just far enough for her leash to pull taut in her master's hand. Palooka coughed and spat and checked his watch—nearly 1:00 a.m. Just enough time to catch their fight, but far past when he would have liked to be in bed.

Sometimes Silver made Palooka nervous: the way her black fur disappeared in the shadows of the alley, her white streaks floating like torn paper strips, her face cut in half down the middle, leaving one blue eye abandoned and seeming to float in the air as if attached to nothing. She stood in ghostly pieces. Palooka almost hated Silver's one white leg, which appeared as a bone and seemed to prop her up on an impossible and uncanny point of balance, but he'd rather her do her business here than down and across the street by the boxing hall, where the road declined and sagged nearly into the river bank. There, dogs rarely left the hall to do anything other than bleed out.

Silver emerged from the alley, whole again under the street lights, and turned her nose to the air, sniffed, and waited for her master to lead the way. After cracking his knuckles under his chin (an old habit) and unwinding a bit of Silver's leash, Palooka crossed the street and walked toward the boxing hall with Silver directly beside him. By the time they were only two blocks away, Palooka could hear and smell the inside: dogs yelping, and the stench of the dirtied floor—so much different than years ago, a lifetime, when the young son of a butcher mopped nightly, leaning on the cords of the ring and hoping maybe Palooka would finally offer him a beer for his hard work.

The outside of the hall had held up better than the other buildings on the block (with the old sign—Seismic Senter!—only slightly crooked), and the windows were still in-tact despite being boarded up. Every other place around here from the deli to the tavern was either officially condemned or outright abandoned. The river had risen over the years and slowly eaten away the foundations of the road, pulling everything toward itself in a patient, decade-spanning meal. The main difference of the boxing hall was its front door, which was now painted black and guarded by a man named Oswin, its gatekeeper, who upon seeing Palooka and Silver nodded and lit a cigarette.

"Hey, the Geezer's finally here," said Oswin, his voice a deep bass line reciting another of Palooka's many names. He was a factory of a man with pink scars crisscrossing his arms and vampire bats tattooed on his neck. "You're late, I'm pretty sure."

Palooka said he knew and reached for the door's handle, but Oswin stepped in front of it. A gatekeeper wouldn't be necessary if not for the animals lurking in this place—some of them more vicious than the dogs. Despite Oswin trying to monitor who could and couldn't come inside, scum tended to find its way in and stick like barnacles: men with no dogs of their own, only looking to spectate, pacing between fights and waiting to satiate some kind of bloodlust. Foolish ones sometimes challenged Oswin for entrance when they had no cash or fighter of their own—anyone inside either needed to own a dog, be a dog, or bet on a dog. Whether they flashed a knife, offered a bump, or simply tried to push past, Oswin took these notions as insults, grabbing men and taking them out back to the river, where he'd hold their heads under, bring them up, then down again, until they begged for him to stop. But he never turned away someone known to have decent money, no matter what they did inside. By all means, he'd say, enjoy the show. Place bets with Weldon. He's the wiry dude over there.

"I'm just gonna say the odds don't look great," said Oswin, towering over Palooka and flicking his cigarette's ash toward Silver, where it landed on her nose and made her sneeze. "Also saying that I'm not exactly pulling for you, and I hope you're not scared. Weldon's been stalling for you and letting some smaller fights play out." He shrugged and opened the door. "If you want to get her riled or whatever, you've got twenty minutes." Oswin gestured to the back corner where owners provoke their fighters with cattle prods and makeshift whips. Palooka shook his head and wound Silver's leash more tightly around his hand. He walked inside.

Palooka could never get used to the place, despite the layout of the room being the same as it had always been: the ring in the center, scattered workout equipment, card tables here and there. To the old boxer, the hall now stood like a familiar yet muddled memory. Instead of the customary ropes, a chain-link fence surrounded the ring, and the workout equipment had been either dismantled or shoved into corners. No athletes walked the floors, and no polka played from the jukebox, but dogs ran wild and people had to yell to be heard over the barks.

Back in his day, when he was someone who trained five nights a week and brought his own gloves, the hall wasn't orderly by any means, to be fair. The red-faced, poker-playing, Polish adhesive of the city used it practically as a dance hall, and Palooka had been more likely to join a rigged game of Omaha than he'd been to find an opponent who wasn't buzzed on Bock lager. But the stupid smiling drunkards weren't always stupid smiling drunkards. They loved to watch him, to challenge him, to sometimes sling on gloves and fight among themselves, and when their draws ended in the river (in icy water endurance tests), they'd forgive each other over shared cigarettes, compare their broken fingers, and ask Palooka for advice on their left hooks. Every now and again, a promising young fighter came in, only for Palooka to knock him down. He had made friends here, for what it was worth, but mostly he fought.

Silver panted and scratched her ear with a hind leg, something Palooka had come to notice as a bit of a nervous tic. When she was in the ring (which she'd survived four times now—her master leading the way home with an envelope of money, his dog cover in blood), she was tactile and quick, rarely hesitating. When she saw other dogs fight and kill each other, Silver acted like a rattled puppy, whining and scratching and looking toward the door. Palooka had learned to pull on her leash harder and bring her closer to the ring. After seeing a couple fights, she usually calmed down.

Presently, in what Palooka assumed was one of the stalling matches, two pit bull competitors tore into one another with fierce speed. One dog lashed into the other, attacking at a hind leg. Silver whined again but finally sat as Palooka watched the fighters closely. He imagined their hind legs elongating and bending and standing tall in tightly-laced shoes, their bloody snouts shrinking into split lips. They did not bite but punched and danced around one another with the patience of experienced fighters. Palooka saw himself up there, a challenger, and he picked his opponent: the giant outside.

And he could see it so clearly: himself bobbing from right foot to left, saluting, crowd cheering—Oswin across the ring, backing against the ropes like he's on the edge of something deep. This is an unfair fight, and everyone knows it, because Palooka has the build, the smirk, the Presley eyes. Hairless hardened forearms, bombs for fists. And Oswin, poor guy, asking can he have a second to stretch his shoulder, to get a drink of water. But the bell doesn't wait for him, doesn't wait for anything, because now Palooka's feet are fast, hands too, green gloves like go-lights—his punches quick and ostensibly light—each jab knocking Oswin nearly off-balance. Oswin manages to find an opening and swings his heavy fist, but Palooka sidesteps and sends the giant flying backward with an arcing uppercut. Oswin slumps on the ropes. Ding ding. Victory. Crowd roars, quiet murmurs from spectators in the corner—you think we'll see him on TV? Palooka hops down, accepts a beer, cracks it open, sings along to Perry Como. All fun and games.

But then someone nudged past Palooka and knocked him in the shoulder. The three ropes around the ring became a chain-link fence, the music faded into narcotic banter, the beer in his hand slithered back into the shape of his cane.

Spectators dispersed from the circle they'd made around the ring. Many of them, mostly those who owned fighters, wore tattered suits and smoked cigarettes out of long filters. That was the joke: find some formal wear in the garbage, pour malt liquor into skinny glasses, ignore what you just stepped in—make all this seem funny. The ones who didn't wear suits sometimes could have been mistaken as normal, but they watched fights enraptured, barely holding back their relief at the sight of a dying dog, like a sickness inside them had been exorcised.

Palooka bit his bottom lip and pulled Silver along. He looked for somewhere they could sit relatively alone, but the hall was packed. Everyone must have known Silver was challenging the Grand Champion, and anyone who hung around this place for more than a night knew dogs never lasted long. Most of the card tables were occupied, so Palooka leaned against the wall. Silver sniffed and walked a small circle before sitting down next to him then stretching out on the floor. She rested her head across Palooka's shoes.

Before long, Weldon approached them. He had the stride of a rushed businessman always headed to a meeting for which he was perpetually late.

"Oldies," Weldon said, "I gotta say, honestly, and don't be mad, but you guys look like Looney Tunes or some shit, standing there like that. Ever watch Looney Tunes? You must've had kids, I'd bet. Or did you watch when you were a kid? But really, it's like, Jesus, the whole boy and his dog act, man's best friend. I don't know what it is, seriously, but I could totally see you guys dropping anvils on each other." Weldon gave everyone shit, but no one got as much as Palooka and Silver. Palooka stood hunched with his pants so high only three buttons of his shirt were visible, and Silver with her windswept mane and iced blue eyes was nothing like her brown-furred opponents.

"So anyway, I really do need to ask you something, Oldies." Weldon smiled, Palooka stared. "People've been talking, and I need to know. Is it true you were on The Little Rascals?" Weldon laughed, the sound of a stuttering engine, and Palooka waved him off. "No, really! My grandma loved that shit. Come on, Oldies!" Weldon shook his head. "At least sit down or something. You look like you're about to keel over. Jesus."

Weldon approached a group of men in spectators' seats, an official name for stolen office chairs. He procured a chair and rolled it toward Palooka. Someone had patched it with duct tape to repair the spots that dogs had chewed. Weldon kneeled down and scratched a dog underneath the chin, snatched a beer from a nearby table, and disappeared into the crowd.

Palooka sat and took a granola bar out of his pocket. A group of men in faded velvet suits passed by with their razors in one hand and plastic bags in the other and entered the restroom. Another group, gathered nearby on the floor, took out their glassware and papers. Some walked past and acted like they were going to hit Silver, but the dog never flinched. Some tossed their flasks, others clinked their bottles before smashing them on the floor. Everyone but Palooka spent their time between fights getting as fucked up as possible, mostly because it was too easy to drop a beer or spill a bag during the heat of a good match. Palooka broke his granola bar into four small pieces. His stomach hurt if he ate too fast.

Nearby, two dogs leapt at each other. A small crowd gathered and treated the off-stage fight like any other, yelling commands: rip him to pieces, tear him to shreds. Both dogs' chain leashes were still attached to their collars, their owners nowhere to be found. They became entangled, and Palooka couldn't tell if the dogs were fighting or struggling to untie themselves until one forced the other onto its back and attacked at the stomach.

The winning dog twisted in its chain until it was free. Oswin pushed through the crowd and removed the one lying there, saying something about how off-stage fights needed to broken up as quickly as possible, then took the dog out back, tossed it down the hill, and left it there to be discovered by riverbank critters. Those who had been watching dispersed as if nothing happened. The winning dog skittered in a brief craze before Oswin returned, grabbed its leash, and drug it toward a table where he tied the chain and left the dog.

Palooka smiled as he watched the events unfold. This place did not bother him, and his enemies did not phase him, even when they walked by and tried to intimidate him and his fighter—"Your bitch is dead meat." He ignored them. The ring was his home and its rules were simple: winners and losers, the strongest survived. He patted Silver's head and smoothed her ears over, not something he did often. She remained still. Sometimes he didn't know what he liked more: that she was strong or that she obeyed. As Palooka stood to ready Silver for their match, even though his back cricked and his hand's grip tightened on his cane, he was confident there was nothing they could not do.

"Yo, Bones!" Palooka's opponent called from a distance. "You still with us? I think I see some drool on your lip." Palooka repositioned his glasses and saw the enemy, Nat Bartola, the richest man thus far in the operation. Nat pointed at Palooka and smoked a cigarette through a long, pink filter. Having started the whole formal wear fad, the high society make-believe, Nat wore an unusual bright green suit, and most of the men here, if not in his immediate circle, were just copycats, poor imitations, hoping that perhaps by dressing like him, their dogs might survive.

Next to him, sitting like a gargoyle, was Apollo, the pit bull Grand Champion. Nat kicked Apollo every few seconds and tightened the fighter's chain leash. Apollo was battle-scarred and hyperactive. The dog looked from side to side with energized alertness and flung his slobber onto Nat's shoes. Apollo had a sigma shaped scar on his chest just below his throat, a personal touch from his master.

Weldon announced the fight would be starting soon and called for Palooka and Nat to enter the ring. Someone let out a loud howl. Palooka coughed and hacked up mucus into his handkerchief, and Nat cried for someone to call an ambulance.

"Silver." Palooka's voice was hoarse. He realized he had not often said her name aloud. Silver looked up at her master. Above her left eye was a scar from a previous fight. Her flesh was exposed and the fur had never grown back. It made her seem surprised, but also secretive, or in on a joke. And as Palooka entered the ring and looked around him at the men and their dogs, he wished they would all run away. He wished the room was empty, that his trembling hands had not betrayed his strength, that the ugly dogs had not dirtied his own, that this ring had not become a place for the hounds.

The foes stood opposite one another: Nat and Apollo, Palooka and Silver. Weldon walked around the ring and read fake ground rules from a piece of paper, joking about no sucker punches. "I want to see a clean fight, boys."

Silver sat still, her leash undone. Apollo pulled on his chain, and Nat strained to hold him. Weldon read off the stakes as they stood: 80:20 in Apollo's favor. Palooka thought about petting Silver before leaving the fighter's side, maybe assuring her that the numbers didn't matter.

"What's your dog's name again, Bones?" Nat tried lighting a cigarette but could not keep his arm steady while also holding Apollo's chain. "Wasn't me who named him Apollo, you know. Just something some drunk said back when I first bought him." He paused and squinted, finally managing to light his cigarette. "Barely even remember what he said, but must've been good enough to stick." He knocked his fist against Apollo's skull as if on wood for luck.

Weldon rang the bell, and Nat undid Apollo's chain. The animals flew into one another and knotted. Palooka and Nat exited the ring, Nat with a swagger, Palooka with a limp.

Apollo leapt back from Silver then thrashed forward, attacking the husky's neck. Though she managed to shake him off, Apollo threw himself into her again, this time knocking Silver over and sending her sprawling toward the corner of the ring, where she planted her legs and shook her head. She was already panting.

Nat and his suited posse laughed and talked and smoked, as if they didn't care who won. "At least her fur's pretty," said Nat, seemingly to no one in particular. Then, turning to Palooka, as Apollo charged toward Silver, "Hey, Bones, what do you think? Think my dog's ugly?"

Palooka did not respond—he was with Silver: seeing through her glacial eyes, spying the ring's other three corners, smelling something foul and primal and looking for an escape route because here came Apollo again, and faster than expected, hurtling his brown, hulkish body practically on top of Silver and tearing into her ear, leaving it to hang like a tattered flag. Palooka felt the blood run down her neck and sensed her panic when Apollo charged yet again and forced Silver onto her back. She rolled with her paws in the air. A gouging bite to Silver's defenseless throat would be enough, Apollo's abnormal largest fang doing its work, but Silver righted herself and dashed to the other side of the ring.

"Bad idea," said Nat. He looked to Palooka. "She might be quick, but you don't run from Apollo."

Apollo snarled and took an offensive stance. He wasn't faster than Silver, just larger, broader, so that each time he chased Silver to another of the ring's corners he overtook her easily, knocking her over like a ram.

Finally, Silver struggled to stand and lay still, crumpled against the chain-link wall. Apollo wasted no time and bit into one of Silver's legs, ripping her flesh and spilling her blood onto the ring.

"Nobody teaches fight like that," said a man standing near the wall, eyeing Nat and his group.

"Some kinda strategy there. Like unnatural shit," said another. Palooka had heard that Nat trained his dogs to torture their opponents. Apollo had chosen not to approach, despite having the chance to attack Silver's neck and end the fight.

A group of spectators, deeming the fight essentially over, left the crowd and walked toward Weldon, calling for their money. Palooka's hands trembled and he could not steady his breath. He thought of Silver lying there: dead, a victim to the beast, another dog thrown out the back door and into the river.

But Apollo spent too much time in one place, and Silver managed to twist and scratch her opponent in the eye. Apollo stumbled back, shook his head, licked his chops. Silver rose and looked at Palooka. Stringy flesh hung from one of her legs.

Meanwhile, someone snuck behind Palooka and began messing around with him, nudging at his cane and sprinkling dirt on his shoulder. Before Palooka could walk away, someone else joined in and took the old man's cane outright. Palooka lost his balance and landed on his knees, and when he found he could not stand, he crawled to the stage's edge and grabbed at the fence. A cold pain flooded into his legs, patient and numbing, but he found Silver's eyes and began to pull himself up. He heard Weldon's voice from somewhere behind him, shooing the men away and demanding the cane, but being this close to the ring—Palooka wanted to be up there, wished he could pull the fence apart and touch the fighters.

Silver flashed her fangs and attacked, nails clacking as she soared into Apollo. Her teeth lodged, gnawed, ripped. Someone from the crowd grabbed at Silver's hind leg, so she turned and bit into the hand, a scream of pain ringing out as she spun again—a zebra blur—and faced Apollo, who panted and slobbered.

"You're gonna get blood all over you," said Weldon from behind Palooka, holding the old man's cane. When Palooka reached out to grab it, Weldon pulled it back. "Are you all right?" For once, Weldon appeared sober, unfrenzied. "You look a little dizzy, Geezer, I'm not gonna lie."

Before Palooka could respond, one of the dogs cried out, followed by the sound of broken glass. Spectators had begun to climb the ring's fence and throw trash at the dogs. They performed this strange ritual whenever a fight seemed particularly even. One threw a jagged glass pipe and hit Silver in the eye; another spilled a cup of cold tobacco spit and spoiled beer on Apollo. The Grand Champion shook his body back and forth, distracted for a moment. Silver's left eye was a darkened slit, but she found Palooka with her right. Weldon dropped Palooka's cane and jumped onto the fence, his arms and legs sprawling crooked and spider-like. He sometimes tried to commentate fights when he thought they were nearing the end.

"Here's the best part, folks," said Weldon. At first, he'd managed to make his voice somewhat audible. "These great fighters, you hate to see just one walk away. Where I'm from we call these slobber-knockers, fights where it's back and forth and back and forth—" but his rambling eventually joined the snarling and screaming of the men and their dogs.

Silver ran into Apollo and knocked him down, showing her teeth and moving in toward her opponent's now upward-facing snout. Palooka reached out toward the fence, looked at Apollo, noticed desperation he'd seen in panicked fighters before—a giddiness in movement, a fidgeting in the limbs like a beetle on its back. Surprised by Silver's strength, Apollo's dollish, obsidian eyes darted back and forth, looking for a way to escape but, before he could right himself, Silver bore her teeth into his neck, and his eyes rolled over pearl.

Nat shook his head. The fallen Grand Champion's cries joined the cheers and tantrums of the crowd as Silver's head jerked back and forth, mauling. Palooka tasted the blood and relished in Apollo's wails, smiling when they finally subsided in a deep gargle.

And the old man saw it all, how it could be.

How he could run up to the ring and pump his fist in the air, Silver running small congratulatory laps around Apollo's corpse, Nat entering the ring and crying over his fighter's dead body, Palooka patting him on the back, consolatory for a lesson learned. The cheaters and monsters, they come too, and shake the old man's hand. Jack Weldon jumps onto the stage, "Whatta fight!" and opens his arms wide. "No earnings, Geezer. No money at all—just take the whole damn place. It's yours." Oswin opens the front doors and lets in light. For a moment, the windows are unbroken, the yellow tile floor is empty, a soft song plays from the old jukebox that Palooka can actually hear, because there are no more fights, no more barks—no more dogs at all.

"Oldies, could you get your dog and split?" Weldon said to Palooka, standing isolated and staring at the ceiling. "We've got another fight to get going and—oh. Here's the money." He handed Palooka an envelope. "It's not a lot. Not that it wasn't a big deal to beat Apollo, honest to God, congrats—the bets did show 80:20, I swear. But people weren't all that interested I guess. Not much money behind the fight. Really though, seriously badass shit. Quite a pup. Buy her a big red steak, those kind from the cartoons." Weldon walked away and disappeared into the crowd.

Two men in suits dragged Apollo out back and tossed him down the hill. Oswin walked Silver to Palooka and said something about her being black, white, and red all over. The old man grabbed Silver's leash and looked to Nat, who handed someone money and took a new pit bull on a rope. He walked toward Palooka.

"There's a little doggy bed out back for the ones that die slow," said Nat, passing by Palooka and bumping him in the shoulder. The old man swayed and took uncertain steps, his pain returning to his knees and reaching from his toes to his thighs. He held his breath when his legs locked altogether, past injuries filling him like phantoms: a night when he had drunk with the card-players, forgotten to tie his laces, tripped in a match and broken an ankle; or was it the kickboxer who had challenged him, had become frustrated and attacked his shins, had said old-school boxers weren't shit.

Palooka looked at the floor—littered with red, smeared pawprints, where Silver panted and her blood scrawled a pattern of its own—then toward the front door but could not spot Oswin, could not see a way out. Somewhere in the back, Nat whipped a dog with a cord and laughed loud enough to be heard among the animals, yelling for someone to get him a drink or so help him god.

Palooka stumbled. He took a step forward and his cane caught in a nook, snapping slightly at its midpoint and bringing him to the ground. An explosion in his knee—his vision tunneling and pulsing. He checked to make sure his glasses had not fallen off (What's with Oldies?) and looked for his dog, for Silver, who licked his hand (This dude gonna die or?) as if to say, "Here I am."

Palooka rose with his right hand, his left fluttering and confused and barely holding the dangling piece of his cane. He wrapped Silver's leash around his wrist but would not walk, only stood, blinking, moving his lips up and down like he was about to speak. Silver sensed panic and led her master out of the havoc, weaving the old man through, her three working legs rattling as they carried their dead-weight fourth.

Near the entrance, Palooka stopped to look at a light fixture above that teetered back and forth while Silver pawed at the door. She turned around and barked at Palooka and, when he did not respond, nipped at his shins to urge him to move. Oswin eventually saw them and opened the door, saying something to Palooka to which the old man did not respond. Instead, Palooka coughed and spat, his phlegm smacking near Oswin's shoes, and as the door closed behind him he barely heard someone say, "Hey, who's fightin' next?"

Outside, Silver sniffed at the sidewalk, pulled on her leash, and led her master the way she thought to be home, her tired paws ticking with limp-like arrhythmia. The streetlights shined a lazy orange that made her sleepy. Each time the old man stopped, she whined and barked and pleaded with him to please keep going. After only a couple blocks, Palooka untied her from his arm and looked out at the river. Silver picked up her leash and held it in her mouth and dropped it at her master's feet, but he did not seem to notice.

Palooka looked at the black waves that ate themselves in slow, repetitive procession. He wanted to throw a stone but was cautious for swimmers settling a draw. He heard his dog sniffing at his shoes and looked down at the stupid thing, Silver's eye asking him questions about where they would go. He kicked her. She backed away, confused. He kicked again. She answered with an unsure whimper. He struck. She howled. When the old man made his way down the slope to the bank, Silver followed.

Palooka spotted a fallen tree near the water and made his way toward it, finally sitting down and resting his forehead in his hands. Silver kept her pursuit and stood before him, strands of skin latched to one leg like angel hair pasta, her fur damp and reddening, one eye a swollen black-maroon mess. Palooka ignored her. He hadn't looked so different years ago, punching out a heavyset barkeep, staggering from the ring with fast-forming bruises and a bloodied chin. But no, he was remembering wrong, surely it had been different.

Palooka threw his broken cane at Silver. She picked it up and brought it to his lap. He coughed and cursed the dog and threw the cane far. Silver followed and returned it. He threw rocks and empty cans and old moss-covered things. Silver retrieved them all. He coughed and threw a stick, this time caught and carried by the river. Silver tried to follow it, but collapsed. After some time, she rose and retrieved it where it had shored, only for the old man to throw it again. Silver went back and forth, waiting for her master to tire of this game.

Wily and Strange and Rough Around the Edges

A Conversation with Shane Page

The following conversation was conducted by managing fiction editor James McNulty.

JM: Hey, Shane. Thanks for agreeing to this talk and working with us to publish your phenomenal story. It's a challenging story, so I'm excited to see how people react to it; I'm also looking forward to hearing you talk more about it. Ready to jump in?

SP: I'm ready!

JM: Let's start at the beginning. Could you talk a little about how you initially conceptualized the story—both how it came into creation and the path it took to our submission inbox?

SP: So there's that old saying that goes something along the lines of, "you've gotta write one-hundred bad stories before you hook a really good one," and I think this story was my 101st in that regard. I wrote "Her Noble Face" five years ago, when I was enrolled in the first writing class that really got me excited about short fiction and had me thinking about stories pretty much 24/7. I think that's why this story has always been so close to my heart. I wrote it during such a fun, challenging, and interesting time in my writer life. Everything about reading and writing felt new and mysterious. So this story always stuck with me, through years of sending it out, revising, sending it out, revising—I always believed in it.

As for the conceptualization, I came up with plots back then by thinking of a character, giving them something they cared about more than anything in the world, then making them confront a sort of bastardized version of whatever that thing was. During an exquisite corpse exercise with some friends, I wrote a line about an old man walking his dog, and over time that old man became a prideful, retired boxer, and the dog became Silver, the stoic fighter.

JM: If that was your typical method of creating plots, is it safe to assume that conformation to a bastardized love is a relevant topic in your own life?

SP: Not really, no. I can't emphasize enough how much the writing of this story was just like a huge learning process—a way for me to ask questions about storytelling and try to answer them. So that idea, the darkened, mirrored passion, was just a way for me to explore conflict and to learn how to put characters into extreme situations. Back then, I thought a story could only be emotionally resonant if it was intense, and to be intense it needed to be dark, and for it to be dark, it needed to be violent, etc, etc.

I don't think along those lines anymore—that stories need to be intense or violent. But the early drafts of this story were, if you can believe it, even bloodier than this one (I think Silver bit off someone's fingers in one draft). I don't really know if I could write a story like this nowadays. I think I write much quieter stories now.

JM: I think violence is an important topic for us to breach with regards to "Her Noble Face." In your mind, how does extreme violence avoid coming off as sensationalistic, and how do you successfully walk the line between showing something horrible and not alienating the reader?

SP: The biggest part, I think, is understanding the story you want to tell. I didn't want to just tell the story of a dogfighting ring, and I didn't want to just tell the story of whether Silver wins or loses her fight against Apollo. The more nearsighted a story is, the more likely it is to rely on violence and to snap its fingers in the face of the reader and say, "Hey, look over here! I'm still interesting!"

I knew Palooka needed to change, and that he needed to realize that what he might understand as a fighting spirit, or a passion for competition, is really a delusion. He is just as terrible as the other owners who subject their dogs to the ring. He's just as senseless as the fighters themselves. When I finally had a clear idea of what Palooka needed to go through, it was easier to cut back on the violence and to not rely on it. I think in early drafts especially, it was tempting for me to rely on shock value whenever I felt like other parts of the story weren't quite working, or where the actual writing itself was difficult. I'd think, "Well, I can't really decide what to do in this scene. Maybe I'll write something obscene or gruesome to keep things spicy."

JM: But then you'd be giving in to sensationalism. Sensationalism is shallow attention-grabbing for its own sake; if the violence is warranted by the story, and if it doesn't go out of its way to draw attention to itself, the violence seems more justified—not sensational. You mentioned that Palooka needed to realize his delusion. Is that your understanding of his final actions at the end in throwing the stick ad infinitum?

SP: In the final scene, I think he is in the process of realizing it, but he's still in denial. He's set in his ways. I think Palooka is a somewhat "dangerous" character *because* he's not in it for the money like the others. You've gotta wonder if he's just waiting for Silver to bleed out so he can head back to the ring with a new fighter. For Silver, as the last line says, there's this hope or belief that her master is eventually going to stop throwing this stick and they can just go home. For Palooka, there's this disbelief, this rejection of what has happened and what is happening.

JM: You spoke earlier about how the story has become less violent with each draft. When the story was submitted, both the protagonist and the title also had a different name. Could you talk a little about what they used to be and how you landed on the current names? The story went through about five rounds of edits with us; can you share with our readers what changed in the course of these revisions?

SP: The original title of the story was "In the Company of Wolves," which I had actually just stolen from an Incubus song (and not even a very good one!). For some reason, this story was always difficult to name, but when you suggested that I find a different title, I started to re-read some of the stuff that had originally helped me write this story, most notably "The Pugilist at Rest" by Thom Jones (I also decided to read some of Katherine Dunn's boxing journalism to get myself into the zone). There's a line in that story that begins, "Besides the deformities on his noble face..." and when I read that, I was like, okay, maybe this is what I'm going for— I could use that line as a title to reference Palooka. Though as we talked more, I looked back at the story and noticed all of the times I described Silver's eyes and face, specifically at the end of the story when she's looking absolutely terrible and Palooka sits there trying to convince himself that she doesn't look so bad, and that he probably looked worse at some point or another. I realized that so much of the story's description is about Silver, and while Palooka is falling apart on the inside, it's Silver who takes the actual beating. So I landed on "Her Noble Face," a title that calls Silver to mind as something special, and beautiful, that by the end of the story is ruined.

As for Palooka's name, he was originally Geezer,

which I envisioned as just another one of the many nicknames that guys around the ring gave to him. I see him as a joke and a common enemy for the people there. They see him as ridiculous and, like the dogs, as not really something worthy of total respect. Anyway, we talked about how perhaps he could be named something a little more specific, less cliché, which was difficult for me because he had been Geezer for five years. I really felt like he couldn't be named anything else... until I considered Palooka, which I think works in a few good ways. I mean, on one hand, a palooka is a shitty fighter, but you've also got Joe Palooka, who was this comic strip hero, so I thought there would be some fun ways to work with the name—Palooka, who used to be a great boxer, is now just some weak old man, and he's definitely no hero. So then, with changing Geezer's name to Palooka, I thought, okay, maybe Weldon gave him the nickname, because Weldon is already referencing *Looney Tunes* and cartoon steaks, and Palooka himself might even be familiar with the *Joe Palooka* comic strip. I ended up thinking this nickname would degrade him more than Geezer would, while also having a few fun connotations.

JM: I'm glad pushing you a little helped you land on better names. The story does seem to have a long history. You noted a few times in the course of our work together that this story has existed in your mind for so long that it was difficult to plug back into the character in revision. Could you explore that idea a little more—how time can divorce us from our work? What pros and cons does that offer?

SP: For this story specifically, I tend to think of it as being written almost by an entirely different writer. I like it a lot, and revising it was challenging and enjoyable, but like I said above, I don't think I could come up with this story nowadays. One of the pros of time is that you understand your work better and, hopefully, you can revise a story in a way that *finally* captures what you always wanted to do. A con, though, for me anyway, is this weird feeling of "What's going on here? What did I want for this scene? How come I don't write like this anymore?" Like I told you over email, I was actually really anxious while revising this story.

JM: You were anxious because you feared you wouldn't be able to capture your original intentions for the story again? I'm having a hard time parsing out what the difference is between your pro and con. On one hand, you're happy that a revision—years later—can allow you a more objective look so you can help the story succeed, yet on the other hand you're worried about staying true to your original intention ("What did I want for this scene?"). It sounds like there's a push and pull between what you think will objectively make the piece better and what you initially wanted for it. Am I understanding that correctly? Is it good to be loyal to the initial vision, or should you allow the piece to grow with you through revision?

SP: You're understanding it! I think what I meant was, I have a really hard time finishing stories if I feel unfamiliar or detached from what I wanted to accomplish. Sometimes this happens if I don't finish something in as little as a couple weeks, and sometimes it happens if I've set something aside for six months. The "con" is really just stress I feel when I try to approach a piece again without being in love with it, and being a little bit afraid that, even if I force myself to finish a draft, it's gonna be scuffed up and lame and not very exciting.

I get so attached to my first/early drafts because I'm a slow writer, so even by the time I've written ten pages, I feel like I've already grown with the piece, you know? I think you should always let the piece grow over time, and when revising, you should always look at the work as the person and writer you are *now*, not the person and writer you were *then*. The anxiety comes in when I start wondering, "Sure, but was I a better writer then? Did I have better ideas? If I work on this story more, am I going to lose what made it special?"

And I think the answer to all of those is no, but it's hard to see that sometimes. I'm also just lazy with revision. I've only just recently stopped hating rewriting stuff. The revision process with you guys helped me finally get over that. I was able to take a deep breath and say, "The old draft isn't going anywhere. It's okay to write a new beginning." Then I'd click back into the old document to make sure it was still there, and it was. So even though it's been a slow process, I've finally been converted to the religion of revision (I don't mean to sound like an after-school PSA for healthy writing habits). I can finally swallow my pride and say, "Yeah, this draft was good, but it was good three years ago. It's time to rework this." I have so many stories sitting in my desk that I haven't touched because I'm afraid to change them and ruin how perfect they are in my head. But how perfect it is in my head isn't what it really is, and that's okay.

JM: I think it's a very popular trend in the literary community to make small revisions rather than large ones; there seems to be an insecurity in many writers, especially rookie writers, where they think that rewriting means their first draft was a failure. I'm constantly reminding writers that Raymond Carver rewrote his stories over twenty times. That doesn't mean his earlier drafts "failed"—the stories just weren't complete yet. Let's refer to evolution as a metaphor here: a caterpillar becomes a butterfly, but that doesn't mean the caterpillar was a failure. I'll often read submissions that clearly haven't gone through more than one significant draft—the polish on the sentence-level isn't there, and the body of the story isn't filled out yet. Scant paragraphs are often a red flag in that regard—they signal that the writer hasn't yet filled out their story.

SP: Well, revision can look so different for every story and for every writer. Sometimes all the major work happens in your head, and sometimes it happens in the actual writing, but other times you need to do a bit of one before you can do the other. You always need to ask yourself: what's keeping the story *out*? Why does this draft not let the story *in*?

So what I mean is, for one example, it's common for most newer writers to have to clean up sentences, to work on paragraphs, etc., but when a teacher or editor points out these technical errors to a student or writer, I think what they're really trying to do is cut aside the brush and show the writer where their story is hidden. Yeah, a vague description is something any writer can clean up, but you clean up that sentence to get a better look at the story, and maybe you realize now that the protagonist is never in any tense situations. What if the stakes are unclear, or the pacing is weird, and the story is just hard to get into? Those types of questions are what make revision so challenging, especially for younger writers, because you can't just move around a couple commas. But I think the hope is something similar to when you've lost something in your house, and as you go around looking for it you end up tidying random stuff, maybe even reorganizing some things. You eventually find the thing, and now your house is a little cleaner.

Other times it's the opposite. I've personally had a lot of trouble with drafts that are written fine. The language is fun, the structure works, there's not anything immediately noticeable that's pushing the story out. The problem is that somewhere between a bunch of pretty sentences, a story didn't really happen. So the initial work for revision on a draft like this really should be nowhere near the original writing. It should be in asking questions about the characters and trying out new scenes and being willing to write it all over again from the start. This time, you've decided to just stop looking for the stupid keys and go for a walk.

With this story, though, the major plot points stayed the same through revision—what happens in the story has always been what happens, the tensest moments have always been right where they are. But I think one of the most significant things you guys pointed out for me in our early drafts, which both changed and improved the story drastically, was definitely the shortcomings of the language. I actually don't have a very good vocabulary (except for a handful of ACT words in my back-pocket), so a lot of times I feel like I have to vary my writing style from story to story to make up for what I feel I lack in word choice. I thought you and your editors did an amazing job of showing me some of the weak points in my writing style, specifically helping me make descriptions more concrete, but you also never told me explicitly what to do, which made me face my demons, in a way.

JM: I've always abided by the dictum that an editor's job is only to show you the problems, not show you how to fix them; as you say here, that method forces you to learn rather than simply be corrected. It's also not the editor's place to write the story for the writer—even slightly.

SP: I was forced to change my old writing and actually think about what I was trying to make the reader *see*. I don't think I've really thought about description that intensively since I first started writing almost ten years ago. I used to write a sentence then compare it to whatever book I was reading at the time, and I'd make myself rewrite it until I could copy people's styles. I haven't done this in almost seven years, but I'm pointing it out because I've always been conscious of style. This practice had a lasting effect on me because, to this day, whatever book I'm reading has a direct influence on my writing. When I had to read *Ulysses* for a class at school, none of my writing made any sense and was pretty much insufferable.

JM: A Joyce imitation? That *does* sounds irritating, but I think that's how most writers start out: emulation. You become an artist—be it a writer, painter, filmmaker, etc.—because you love the artform, so of course you'll at first emulate who you love; those artistic loves are your first teachers. Have you had any luck pulling away from that accidental mimicry? Or do you embrace it?

SP: I embrace it because I can't really stop it. With the *Ulysses* example, the result was horrible, and when I was reading *Jane Eyre*, you know, I kept trying to build up to my "Reader, I marred him" moment. It really gets that bad! I can't get a writer's style out of my head, and sometimes it's something I have to pull away from because I end up looking silly.

Sometimes it really works out, though. About a year ago, one of my teachers loaned me the short story collection *Manual for Cleaning Women* by the late Lucia Berlin, and by imitating that book both on purpose and through osmosis, I felt like I re-learned how to write short stories. I had been in a *major* slump. I hadn't really finished a story in almost a year and a half, and I didn't feel confident in my writing whatsoever. But when I started to read Berlin's collection, I felt like I was learning everything all over again—the characters were complicated but relatable, and their conflicts were clear but nuanced. Even the way Lucia Berlin describes things felt entirely new (Lydia Davis discusses this in the book's forward for a little bit, but then you see Berlin's descriptive language in action, and it's so much fun to read and to imagine). So in this case, I feel like emulation brought me out of one of the most difficult phases I've had as a writer. I was excited to write again and felt like I could do it.

JM: What writers were you reading when you wrote "Her Noble Face" that influenced the story? I know you mentioned Thom Jones earlier. Anyone else?

SP: I mentioned being in a writing class that got me pretty jazzed about short fiction, and on one hand I was reading just a bunch of essential short stories that have stuck with me over the years. "Car Crash While Hitchhiking," "Tenth of December," "Brownies"... I was reading like a madman back then. Anything I got my hands on I'd read, and any sentence I liked I'd write down in a notebook, until I had a notebook full of all my favorite sentences from all my favorite stories (I lost this notebook at some point). I remember loving Flannery O' Connor and Brady Udall's stories; the collections *Everything That Rises Must Converge* and *Letting Loose the Hounds* really stuck with me. I remember reading *White Teeth* and *The Crying of Lot 49* and wanting to be able to write books like those. I like plots where there are a lot of moving pieces, with language that feels almost interactive.

JM: Let's circle back to the topic of revision briefly, since that seems to have played such a huge role in this story. I loved how, at one point in our editing session, you sent me back a draft where all the paragraphs had been cleanly spaced so you could analyze each paragraph on its own terms—as a distinct and separate entity. I think this is a brilliant way to edit—a great way to pay attention to each paragraph and sentence to help make them sing. Did you intuitively pick up this method, or was it taught to you?

SP: The paragraph separation thing is just something I have to do to keep my mind straight. When I see all the paragraphs clumped together, I get overwhelmed and can't get a feel for the pacing of the story. I've never really been the type of person to cut up a story into pieces and try moving them around (I know some people who love doing this), but when I revise stories, I definitely look at each paragraph as an individual unit and ask myself what that paragraph accomplishes. Does it take the story anywhere? Does it show the reader a new idea, even if there's no forward plot movement? If the answer to both of those is no, then the paragraph gets axed. I like stories where things *happen*, so if I feel like nothing much is going on, then that's a problem.

I do think that rewriting is still probably the most important thing. One of my writing teachers, who has also been a mentor over the years, told me years ago I needed to become comfortable with rewriting stories from the very beginning. My first reaction to this was like, I'm never going to be able to do that because I'm so attached to my sentences (this same teacher told me to beware of only focusing on *the line*—story stuff needs to be happening too. After a while, no one cares how tricky and clever your sentences can be). But after about three years of ignoring that advice, I think I'm coming around, and revising is starting to be fun.

JM: Let's talk a little about the language and the rhythm of the story. The sentences in "Her Noble Face" seem to sing—the audial rhythm moves well and the sentence structures create a lively dynamic. You spoke before about how to craft a great paragraph. What goes into composing a great sentence?

SP: I don't feel like I've really started writing a new story until I get a feel for what I want it to sound like. I try to imagine how a story would sound if it were telling itself. Obviously some stories are quiet and meditative, and others are a bit more wily and strange and rough around the edges, and, in both those cases, the writing style and tone will reflect those characteristics. But for whatever reason this idea is just so important for me. I have to imagine it as a story's "voice," and I have to get it right before I do any serious extended writing at all.

And I always know when I've hit the voice of a particular story for the first time. I write all of my initial drafts by hand, and eventually I catch the first spark, and I can't really describe it any other way, but when I hear the voice for the first time, I usually stop writing by hand immediately and finish the story from there on my computer. Even if I have all the plot thought out, I have to wait until I find that voice. One reason I do this is because, when I type, I tend to favor run-on sentences, and if I don't have a plan for the style before I sit down, everything's going to be long-winded and awful. Maybe I'm just waiting for some kind of intuition.

As for an individual sentence, that's not really something I've ever given specific thought to. I feel like if I think about it too much, I won't know what to do when I actually sit down to write. I kind of just trust what I'm writing when I'm writing it. Every now and again I might have an idea for something I want to try, like a prose effect, like in the scenes in "Her Noble Face" where Palooka enters these imaginary worlds, the sentences feel a little floatier, a little less hooked to reality, etc., but I feel like everyone does this.

I'll also add that I felt like the style was very important for "Her Noble Face" specifically. I wanted the style to feel like it was reflective of the dog-fighting ring, and of the characters, and, again, as if the setting were telling the story. And I was also anxious about the content—how violent (again, especially early drafts) it was—so I told myself that if I wanted anyone to actually read this, I'd need to write it in a voicey, punchy, fun style. And I do feel like a lot that has been toned down (which is for the best—trust me), and the final version we have here is much more controlled.

JM: I'm glad you didn't get too "voicey, punchy, and fun"; then you'd be guilty of the sensationalism we spoke of earlier. Shifting gears as we start to wrap up, I always like to ask writers if any other mediums influence their writing.

SP: I think music does on a pacing level. I like to imagine a story progressing similarly to a song or an album. And I think movies inspire me often for tone and details. Like sometimes after watching a movie I'll try to make a list of words I think would describe the style of the movie, and I'll try to write in a way that conjures the way the movie looked. But I'm mostly a writer who is influenced by writing and speaking. I don't listen to music when I write because it distracts me, and I can't, you know, like drink and write, or anything like that.

But more than anything, I'm influenced by conversation. Two of my favorite stories I've written were both inspired by stories my friends told me. One time my friend Addie walked into my apartment and said, "Weird day at work!" and she proceeded to tell my roommate and I all about a strange interaction she had with some customers at her serving job, and that sentence became the opening line of a story I wrote called "Angels." And another time, my friend Allyson told me this story about a gas station in Texas that had a bear in a cage outside, and I changed the bear to a raccoon and ended up writing "Amber." So, really, more than anything, I'm inspired by the people around me and the way they speak and tell stories of their own. I love listening to my friends talk.

JM: What are you working on now?

SP: As usual, I'm writing stories sometimes and moping about not writing stories other times. I'm putting a bunch of my stories together for my MA, but I'm trying to start thinking beyond short stories a little bit, even though I love them. I think it would be cool to write something longer, but I still have no idea how anyone conceptualizes a novel. But yeah, other than that, I'm working as a janitor at night, teaching and writing during the day, and trying to eat my fruits and vegetables.

JM: Is there anything you'd like to add as we wrap up this conversation?

SP: Not really! Thanks for talking with me. Maybe I should add that I really do love dogs, and what happens to some of them in this story is not indicative of my feelings about them. Oh, I want to thank my friends Tyler and Alex, for putting up with me bringing new drafts of this story to their dorm all the time and agonizing over deciding on a stupid title, and for them not thinking I was a total weirdo, which I am and was, but they were my friends anyway.

JM: I think that about wraps it up! Thanks for taking the time to talk with me, Shane.

SP: No problem! Thank you for seeing something in the story.

"FOX & BRANCH" | ALEXANDER LANDERMAN

"REGRETS" | ALEXANDER LANDERMAN

Ordinary Psalm with Assassination and Slaughter

Julia Levine

In that basement, before the RCA console,
she stood the hissing iron on the board's end,
away from my father's white collar, and wept,
head in what my mother called colored hands,
weeping the quiet way I had always wanted
to cry, though mine sputtered and spun out
in snot, while hers was rain, a freshet shining
down, and it was astonishing. I had never seen
a grownup cry before, something terrible
must have happened in real life, in black and
white on the TV. His youngest your age, she said
the next day, when it seemed a dream, the way
slaughter sounds in an old language, the one
the first people used to name our lakes
and rivers, though it would be years before
I understood that what does not begin in
tenderness, rarely ends there. At five years,
I knew only what it was to be unwanted,
but no matter how I begged she wouldn't
let me go home with her at night, or even
tell me her first name, though I persisted,
guessing the most rare and lovely sounds
I knew— Petoskey?, her chemically straightened
hair moving all in one piece when she shook
her head, Muskegon?, that silver tooth near
the front if she grinned, Kalamazoo?

INTERVIEW

JULIA LEVINE

What inspired the poem?

This poem was inspired by Gerald Stern's poem, "The Dancing," with it's tremendous exhilaration and everyday objects. As a child of Russian Jews who grew up in Flint, Michigan, I immediately connected to the scene of this gritty midwestern store and these three people dancing like crazy at the end of the war. I did not expect to write about my introduction to racism, but instead focused, as Stern does, on common objects from that time (1968). I started with our old and enormous black and white TV cabinet in the basement, but the poem found itself with the ironing board, the glass coca-cola bottle used for wetting the clothes, and went from there.

What was the hardest part about writing it?

The hardest part was figuring out how much background to include. I love how Stern never mentions the armistice being announced, rather it is implied. I wanted to try something like that with this cleaning woman my parents hired, and her extreme importance to me in a very abusive household. It was really difficult to find a balance between telling too much and not enough, and I wrote multiple endings that were ultimately edited out.

What came easiest when writing this poem?

My sense of innocence about bigotry. I still feel stupid and naieve when it comes to negotiating the sensitivities of history and culture. Though my parents were abusive, they also were strong champions of civil rights. In the poem, it was easy to return to that child's state of mind where you believe everyone is equal and are shocked to find out that the world does not see it that way.

How much revision went into this poem?

This poem has been under revision for over four years now. As I mentioned, there were several different, alternate endings that I cut from the piece.

Who are some of your favorite poets?

At this moment in time, I continue to be in love with all of Brigit Pegeen Kelly's work, Alice Oswald, Brenda Hillman, and Frank Gaspar. I read so much poetry and find so many poems by so many poets that literally pierce me on a daily basis. For this, I feel eternally grateful.

If you had to narrow it down, what three or so books have had the most impact on your writing?

Certainly, *Dark Blonde* by Belle Waring and *Silent Treatment* by Lisa Lewis. I had never read work by women that was so direct and honest, and therefore, at times, so angry. It was freeing in every sense of the word and gave me permission to write about many taboo subjects, including my work as a psychologist for sexually abused children, and my own experiences with sexual assault and violence.

Additionally, these were poets that wrote with tremendous control and restraint, which feels extremely important when you are writing about subjects that contain their own internal explosives.

Brenda Hillmans book, *Bright Existence*, and its companion, *Death Tractates*, were powerful books for me, in the way she explored spirituality grounded in the physical, visceral world. Her exploration of the Gnostic Gospels became a model for me in my current project, which involves writing a series of psalms and various other types of prayers based on ordinary experiences.

How long have you been writing poetry?

I wrote my first poem at age five! My father stopped from his work long enough to type it up on his Selectric, and I was hooked from then on!

Where can readers find more of your work?

I have published four collections of poetry—the most recent, *Small Disasters Seen in Sunlight,* published by *LSU Press* in 2014, was awarded the 2015 Northern California Book Award in Poetry. I also have recent work published or forthcoming in *The Southern Review, Tupelo Press Quarterly, Tiferet, Zone 3*, and *Cumberland River Review.*

ABOUT NATURE

ROY WHITE

the kid gave at most half a shit;
he cared not much for green
if it wasn't bounded by foul lines.
Tornadoes he loved, though,
and great shearing thunder,
and the big waves, when he finally saw the ocean.
Again and again he fed his little body
to the breakers, which spewed him back
with an ogre's careless strength.
It was the most fun he'd had
since he was small enough for a big
sister to drop him down the laundry
chute from the second floor hallway.
But once he heard a shriek and saw Aunt Meg
(someone's Aunt Meg, anyway)
hopping through knee-deep water; someone
was fishing on this crowded beach,
someone had snagged her foot
with a hook. Did the kid ever see the wound?
I don't know...I remember
doughnuts the next morning.
Still it stuck with him, the scream
of helpless pain, of being dragged and torn,
played in heavy rotation in his head
like the story of the guy
who gave out apples for Halloween
with razor blades inside, sharp steel
that shreds from beneath the smooth surface.
Sometimes, now that I have hands
for eyes, I lose track
of the leftover tubs
in the fridge, and then I must
probe with a reluctant finger
the clammy lumps of pasta, or poke
the skin of congealed fat
that covers the stew. It's as bad, almost,
as asking a stranger for help.

INTERVIEW

ROY WHITE

What inspired the poem?

It is autobiographical. The two seeds around which it accreted were probably the fish-hook in the foot and the blind person's trepidation about mysterious leftovers.

What was the hardest part about writing it?

Tone is always a challenge, being unsentimental without being off-putting, trying to be witty without becoming trivial.

Is this poem categorical of your work? Why or why not?

Well, it shares some of my usual obsessions: childhood, blindness, fear of Tupperware, and my habit of making abrupt transitions.

What is your favorite line from the poem or the line you are most proud of?

I don't know about proud, but "Again and again he fed his little body / to the breakers" still gives me pleasure because it is so unassuming and yet is not normal.

Is there anything unique about your personal writing process?

Working with a screen reader is at least unusual. I type and my words are read back to me in a robotic voice. Because I can't see the poem, I often revise by retyping a whole line or stanza from scratch, rather than trying to find the few words I want to change.

How long have you been writing poetry? What has changed from your first poem to your newest work?

I started writing poems four or five years ago. On a stay in Italy, I was trying of think how I could share my experiences as a blind traveler, and lines started coming to me.

One change between then and now is that I have less anxiety about line breaks. At first I was worried about seeming too retro, and sometimes leaned toward disruptive breaks. Now I mostly go with breaks that feel natural, with exceptions for variety or some special purpose.

If you had to narrow it down, what three books have had the most impact on your writing?

One Hundred Years of Solitude, Alice's Adventures in Wonderland, The 1982 Bill James Baseball Abstract.

Based on your personal experience, what advice would you give to other writers?

Not sure anyone wants my advice, but here it is anyway: try not to get discouraged by rejections. I had a piece rejected by twenty-four journals and then picked up by *Poetry Magazine.* Go figure.

Where can people find more of your work?

Thanks for asking. There's a list at my blog (lippenheimer.wordpress.com).

DAYS OF 2000

CRYSTAL STONE

I was never good at swimming / like the rest of my family. That year, / I wore swimmies to keep / my head and shoulders above / the edge. I protected / my barbies / the same way I protected / myself, but my brother still / managed to pull their heads off / and I still managed / to tie their hair into knots / when I meant to untangle it. / Isn't that how life is, / more knots / when we mean to untangle / my hands strands / more often / than they are combs. / When I told him / I didn't think I could love / anyone else / this way again / I meant / that loving him felt like / that day / in 2000 when my lungs / emerged as chlorine waters / I had already gotten out / of the pool / grabbed a carrot / from the garden / decided to go in / but when my brother threw / my Barbie in the water / I didn't notice my arms were bare / I jumped / the water was the foggy horizon / of my last sunset. / My dad was so mad at me / you could've died / what were you thinking? / Not about myself / what I mean is that sometimes / we are so focused / on someone else / we don't notice / we stepped into something / we might not come back from / I don't like pools / for the same reason / I don't like love / they are stronger than my body / the thoughts swim right / out of my head / now I live in a place / so windy / the water at the fountain / blows right out of my mouth / and this, too, feels like a kind / of drowning / gasping for something you need / but can't have / my grandmother / only drank / glasses of milk / what I mean to say is that / she wouldn't be sad / by the fountain / when the water left her / in the wind / or the water wanted to / take her under / where her body / could be bubbles / no, her tongue was pearl white / thick and settled / she would've looked up / adjusted her light-rimmed / soupy glasses / she would have just said no

CAVE

ZACHARY ELLER

I.

Two pools forgetting themselves to each other.

We open our mouths and pour vomit and light
now mother then child, lidless eyes & feathers soft.

I empty ammonite in your diamond vessels.
You carry them to waterfall shrines to be lost. Dark

partner, we pace mirrored twelve-mat chambers
maps touched with charcoal, milk of erasers

identical, apart, wandering insubterrane.

II.

They're emptying the potties onto 39th street
and the smelly cool streams casting painful flecks of light
drain through punctures in His side, into fissures in His hands
end in sediment deposits without fragmenting or waning.

Interview

Zachary Eller

What inspired the poem?

The comfort of losing something into another.

How much revision went into this poem?

The images themselves are mostly unchanged since conception, but many small revisions were made over time.

Is there anything unique about your personal writing process?

Not sure how unique this is, but I pretty much only write inbetween moments of doing some other task—often as an escape from something I don't want to be doing.

How long do you usually spend working on a single poem?

With my writing process being as answered above, after an initial free write inspired by some image or feeling, revisions are made in several-minute intervals over the course of a year or longer, until I can read the poem and not want to change anything.

If you had to narrow it down, what three books have had the most impact on your writing?

Classic Haiku, *Paradise Lost*, and *The Norton Anthology of Modern and Contemporary Poetry*.

How would you personally define poetry?

The nuance and textures of language as a medium of expression.

What drew you to *Driftwood Press*?

Initially, the well organized, visually appealing website, and then the selection of skillful, moving writing.

HOW TO LOSE YOUR HUSBAND

ANNETTE SCHLICHTER

FOR MICHELLE

Do not hide the body.

Do not make friends
with the undertaker. Do not wear your wedding
gown to the wake. Do not scream
at your neighbors' heartfelt
condolences or hearty casseroles.

Do not fry up old home
movies for breakfast. Do not fuck
your sister's husband in your parents' bedroom.
Do not take your niece's baby doll
for the girl's little brother.

Do not binge on butterflies
or TV news about American drone
attacks. Do not bring the knife
to your puppy's furry face. Do not bleed
into the gutter in front of your local supermarket.

Do not dance in a dead man's well-worn
flannel underwear. Do not drop his urn into the dumpster
behind your apartment building.
Do not—ever—scatter his ashes
across your searing skin.

Do not stay home alone after midnight.
Do not lie awake in the dark.
Do not close your eyes.

Don't.

Just go on about your day.
Clip your toe nails.
Pay your rent.
Read a poem now and then.

Falter.
Go.

What inspired the poem?

This is a very important poem for me. Because it was one of the first, maybe the first one, that let me see myself as a poet.

I wrote this poem after the loss of my husband, and I wanted—and needed—to express the intensity of my grieving, the excess of emotions, the raw anger and sadness, the sense of disorientation—a kind of cracking up. At some point after his passing, I had read the short story "Involution" by my former colleague and prose writer extraordinaire, Michelle Latiolais, from her collection *Widow*. In one scene, a young woman is hit by a car because she wants to save a child from an accident but it turns out that what she thought was an infant is a doll. I was very intrigued by the way perception works in this scene; I saw everything happen in great detail, in particular the moment of her misperception, which began to haunt me a bit. I identified with it so much. I felt like I lived inside it for a while, and I took the writing from there.

What was the hardest part about writing it?

Writing through the grieving.

What came easiest when writing this poem?

Grieving through the writing.

What is your favorite line from the poem or the line you are most proud of?

My favorite line is "Falter." I like the simplicity of the line, the purity of the word and how its standing by itself expresses a sense of loneliness and despair. And let me tell the readers who do not speak German a little secret: "Falter" is the German word for butterfly, so I also see and hear the lightness and tenderness of the movement of exquisite wings fluttering when I read it. Writing that line, I began to appreciate my bilingualism as source of imagination instead of seeing myself at a disadvantage because I am not a native speaker of English.

Is there anything unique about your personal writing process?

I work a lot with a Thesaurus and a range of dictionaries, online and in print. Because I am not a native speaker, I have always had this anxiety that my writing in English would never be sophisticated enough. So, originally, the dictionaries functioned as a kind of safety blanket. I thought of them as a tool to "get" the meaning of a word. Meanwhile, I began to enjoy the process of being deferred from one word to another and the effect it had on my writing. I find it very liberating. The moving from word to word, the playing with similarities and differences of sense and sound have become an intricate part of my writing. The dynamic makes me aware, again and again of the openness of language as a system and of the pleasures in the process of writing.

Who are some of your favorite poets?

This is a really difficult question. My taste is pretty eclectic.

Sylvia Plath and Emily Dickinson have always been American favorites. I am currently enjoying work by Claudia Rankine, Amy Gerstler, Fred Moten, Danez Smith, Ocean Vuong, and Marilyn Chin.

On the German-speaking side, I appreciate Rainer Maria Rilke, Paul Celan, and Rose Ausländer, and I am currently reading Durs Grünbein, Nadja Küchenmeister, and Friederike Mayröcker and Ernst Jandl (both Austrian).

How long have you been writing poetry?

I started writing in eighth grade in Germany, where I grew up and lived until 1999, when I moved to California. My German teacher gave us poetry assignments, which I liked very much. At the time, I was very focused on rhyme and rhythm. As a young woman in my twenties, I wrote a lot about love and despair (still do). I have been writing in English since 2012.

Do you work in any other artistic mediums? If so, how do those other genres inform your poetry?

Let's say, I engaged in a different kind of creative writing for most of my life. A professor of Comparative Literature until last year, I wrote academic essays for a long time. I believe that there is a good portion of creativity in scholarly writing, but I got tired of the constraints, the rules of publishing, the type of responses, ideas about "productivity" in the institutional setting. However, that practice of academic writing certainly had an impact: first of all, it prepared me for the discipline necessary to be a writer (I am not claiming it always works!) and trained me to organize my day around writing. I also think that my interest in experimenting with structure in my recent poems is informed by my struggles with the rules of academic thinking and writing. I guess I am exploring the constraints and possibilities of structure from a different angle now.

How would you personally define poetry?

Freedom poured into stanzas?

Based on your personal experience, what advice would you give to other writers?

Write! Don't forget to breathe.

Where can readers find more of your work?

One of my poems was published in *Space & Time Magazine* (#129), another one in the first issue of *Beach Reads* (May 2017), a literary journal produced in Laguna Beach, where I live. And in the summer of 2017, *Ghost City Press* published my "micro chapbook" *Like Love* online.

What drew you to *Driftwood Press*?

I like the breadth of themes and forms and interests. Across the issues I read, I have found many pieces that engaged and moved me. And the interviews are inspiring. For me as a poetic beginner, it is exciting as well as helpful to read about other writers' experiences with the creative process. I am happy to contribute to the conversation.

COPPER IMAGE

JOSHUA SILAVENT

All the old things can still be found
if lost, she's digging in the dirt for toys
buried years ago.
All the old things are now out
of order, she's taking tintypes of arcade games
with broken joysticks.

All the old things breathe under
the black light, hands have ripped out the pay phones
by the cord.
All the old things are still standing
somehow, she's trespassing through abandoned
settlers' homes.

And the railroad trestles that narrow the road,
graffiti the age of rust that remembers who came before,
are still good for hanging
or dangling
your feet off.

And the store with the sign written by hand in black marker,
"Welcome" on the outside, "God bless" from within,
is still where she goes to share a word
and grab a drink
to later drink alone.

All the old things can still be read
front to back, she licks her fingers to
mark the pages.
All the old things can be made new again
like retrofits, the same song and dance
sold to the believer.

Gravel roads from here to her home
captured in the fading copper light—
four-way stop signs and
trees overgrown
and.

INTERVIEW

JOSHUA SILAVENT

What inspired the poem?

This poem is an elegy to my city and the splendid grit of age that shows itself in ever-fewer places as redevelopment turns working-class, industrial neighborhoods into mixed-use complexes of luxury condos and fine eateries.

Many artists abhor nostalgia because they equate it with complacency or contentedness, I suppose, but I like its bittersweet taste and the reminders it brings—the spirit of misfit youth, word-of-mouth education, and analog relics of home and work.

I wanted to capture the decay I was seeing in my city, but with as much gratitude as lament—glad for the old signs of man's chaos and trash and courage and fortitude against the contemporary pretense of safety and conceit of security. And I wanted readers to glimpse, as if seeing an old copper tintype in a thrift shop, the ruins and remnants that sheltered life and light in this city, however now worn, a reminder of the ties pierced by pristine new buildings where no memories exist—a requiem for corrupted but empathetic hearts and minds.

What was the hardest part about writing it?

The hardest part in writing this poem or any other is trusting instinct. I do not subscribe to the notion that creativity is an act of channeling or that words are bestowed from some foreign source upon the vigilante and patient writer. Rather, it seems clear to me that artistic creation, while undoubtedly drawing inspiration from the world outside, forms its shape and consistency from within and then spills out when prompted by a sight, a smell, a sound, a taste, a touch, a thought.

Is the poem categorical of your work? Why or why not?

In some ways, yes, in other ways, no. The subject matter—that is, writing about the people and places in my life (while wary of making a didactic call to arms)—is something I visit frequently.

What is your favorite line from the poem or the line you are most proud of?

The line "And the railroad trestles that narrow the road." I keep coming back to this line because it both characterizes the beautiful decay of my city's working-class birth while also sharing the image of a childlike moment of innocent joy. When was the last time you dangled your feet off a ledge? That feeling never grows tiresome or old for me. And the spacing or breaks in this verse is meant to mimic those dangling legs.

Do you work in any other artistic mediums? If so, how do those other genres inform your poetry?

I wouldn't call it art, but there is a certain creativity in my day job as a print journalist. I do a lot of reporting on poverty and issues impacting working-class communities, which has opened me to a new world of poetic inspiration. Spending the last several years writing about, and in kinship with, homeless individuals, for example, has translated into many, many poems.

Where can readers find more of your work?

Links to my journalism, poetry and music can be viewed at my website (joshuasilavent.wixsite.com/kinship).

COUNTY

JACQUELINE BERGER

Today my students are writing poems
about food, an assignment they hate:
it makes us hungry. But they do
what seems to me their best work.
If they're listening, as I am, to your son's
happy shrieks through the wall—
you and your boy in the visitor's room next door,
first time you've seen him in seven months—
no one mentions it,
though most of them are mothers as well.
One woman writes of French toast,
butter that melts beneath the knife, orange juice,
the year she was safe as a child
living with her grandmother.
Another writes a list of bacons:
maple, hickory, pork, turkey;
gumbo appears in three different poems,
and buttered rice, grits, hot-water cornbread,
the sorrow of crawfish, oysters, melancholy
of sausage, pozole, the tender road back
of corn on the cob, someone gestures eating it,
and the true indignity of granola bars,
not the chewy kind but the dry
that the county provides for snacks—
I'm supposed to hand them out
so everyone gets just one;
they can fill their own plastic cups with water.
Drippings, roux, crabmeat, file powder,
Tabasco, okra, shrimp—
by the end of the poem, the mother,
not high in her room in the dark,
not turning out a daughter for dope,
the mother in a kitchen
cluttered with pots and thick
with steam is mapping the road to home.

EXCAVATION REDUX

TARA ROEDER

tiny fish wiggle through televised miasma,
plant themselves in flesh,
transmitting information.

in formation they are one big fish whispering facts.
you sunk my battleship,
they hiss, spout movie spoilers.

sleepswimming a tightrope,
neon blue description of non-existent
treaties.

like eels they spark electric,
unlikely alliances
embedded in their scales.

the scales fall from your own eyes and you catch
the hover of oceanic rumble,
tectonic plated urgency in theirs.

Erasure of Wikipedia Page on Rollercoaster Tycoon™

RAINIE OET

The player is given control over
an empty plot of land and the player
usually suffers.

(Skin tingling)

Many of the rides that can be built are variations on
water. The player can build
loop-the-loops,

(A wasp banging against the screen, as if trying to move through)

can create their own guests to visit the park
with the Peep Designer, or utilize
webcam to impart
facial features.

(Mouth opening, closing)

The guests are treated as separate entities
and the player keeps track of
their thoughts, and needs

and nausea tolerance.

(I smash the wasp with my palm and it falls straight down into my lap)

Soaked! Wild! Now the player can enjoy more than ever
coping with
sunsets,
the
savage separation
of boredom
without limits.

What inspired the poem?

I played an unholy amount of RollerCoaster Tycoon as a middle-schooler. This is a game about possibility and budgeting, about the erasure of fun as a way to create fun for non-you entities AKA Peeps™. Playing RCT was always about wanting to flatten, wanting to move into the computer. But there's glass there. And it doesn't give. All sorts of distractions crop up when you're playing RCT. It's best to ignore them as best as you can. Once, in my case, that involved killing a wasp against the screen.

What was the hardest part about writing it?

Putting myself back in the mindset of twelve-year-old me, who didn't know they were not a boy, who just wanted everything to be fun all the time and who wanted to feel nothing bad.

Is this poem categorical of your work? Why or why not?

It's the first poem of a manuscript I've been sending out called *Moss on Rollercoaster Tycoon.*

Based on your personal experience, what advice would you give to other writers?

Trust the really weird stuff.

Where can readers find more of your work?

You can find more at my website (rainieoet.com). You can also read me online at *The Yale Review, Press 53*'s Flash Fiction Contest, *Cosmonauts Avenue, Hobart,* and more!

Quincy Hill & Iron Ore

Mary Maroste

1.
I close my hands,
tight, around burnt orange stones
& try to feel the pulse of men who drowned under the earth—

I wanted the sun to touch them under their skin,
I wanted their transparent ribs to expand
& release slime trapped in their bodies.

At dusk, I watch the lake
turn to juice, I watch the sharp grass turn to straw—

naked branches, veins stretched across matte & cool grey,
my grandfather's body filled with white water—

my aunt lays in the sour imprint he made on the hospital bed,
& prays for his soul to become ore
or Michael's gun, or the screws in my father's knees.

Above her head, mercury in a daguerreotype is saying—
"you can feel an animal's life through its flank & a house
through mud in the grooves of the floor"

the image—kudzu climbing through open & empty
windows, its vines haunted by the scent of tarnished silver.

There are too many ferns dying in the forest
& their shedding leaves become a thin rug of brown lace—
the moss wishes it was a lichen, pine trees wish they were a fire.

There are too many shoes in this world,
too many tea pots & chrysanthemums
& children sleeping

under highways, their mother's speaking quietly
pressing their lips against their head—
dear thing, there's nothing I wouldn't pretend to be for you.

Night is tied to the shore like a steel canoe
& garden snakes coil around dry seaweed & faded lupines,
their pear colored stomachs become warm honey under my flashlight—

in a different garden, if I wasn't shaking,
I could have touched them.

2.
A large orange moon in my mouth, burns
a long cold burn, like the memory;

my grandmother's small blue cow
filled with quarters, cracked along the belly,

while I drive south to Columbus in a snowstorm
condensation on the sun roof dripped into my mouth, onto my fingers

I could feel the crack in my voice—
bright, doe eye headlights blurred the sharp snow—

the butterfly wanted to be a bird & actually tried—

this is about cars driving through fresh painted highway lines & giving up.

There will be no symbolic
surrender, my bathtub is overflowing,

& I'm not old enough to understand the feeling—

3.
chlorine & lemongrass & heavy grey air—
my mother's uterus sealed shut in Berlin

by a steel spoon with teeth

& the hospital didn't understand what it meant to be gentle,
or a mother, or giving up a child without a choice.

INTERVIEW

MARY MAROSTE

How much revision went into this poem?

This poem has undergone more revision than any other. I still think I'm working on it in many ways.

What is your favorite line from the poem or the line you are most proud of?

"& prays for his soul to became ore / or Micheal's gun, or the screws in my father's knee."

Who are some of your favorite poets?

Bekian Fritz Goldberg, Iliana Rocha, Natalie Diaz, and Thomas Tranströmer to name a few.

Based on your personal experience, what advice would you give to other writers?

Write what feels real to you; don't distort memory for poetic means; the most beautiful writing comes from things that are important and honest to the writer's experience.

Where can readers find more of your work?

My writing is available from *Jabberwock Review, Winter Tangerine, Dancing Girl Press, Pittsburgh Poetry Review, 3288 Review*, and others!

BODY FARM

JOSHUA OROL

Know that if you turn up chewed
to the bone by coyotes, vulture scattered,
there's probably a man with a pistol and a dog
that found you, but in the lab
getting dark purge fluid on her coat sleeves,
not bothering to plug her nose
because there's a job that needs to be done,
another mother wants answers, and besides
it takes both hands
to brush off the maggots
and read what's hidden,
take from it what you will,
but the workers, researchers, and students,
the bodies—
most of us are women.

Out at the ranch
we lay the donations in the dirt
or on the bed of a truck,
sometimes with a protective cage
or a dull green tarp. Six-months for some,
couple years for most,
we collect the hand and foot bones
each in their own small bag.
They appear wooden, take on the color of the dust.

Most of us are women, and most of us have a husband
who respects our work, but won't talk about death.
I envy my gay colleagues only the conversation

and the possibility of lying hand by hand
with a partner who's not scared of the nothing
who might turn, even in death
and see you
as you marble, then bloat
then flies come out of your pores
and your liver leaks dark wine

and beneath you
the Mother says thank you
and through your fragiled ribcage
pushes a fragrant, tawny bouquet.

INTERVIEW

JOSHUA OROL

What inspired the poem?

An interviewer on my favorite podcast "Criminal," a local reporter from Durham, NC, was fascinated to learn that the overwhelming majority of scientists working with the dead on body farms are women. As a transfemme poet, one of my favorite things to write are persona poems about women doing things that are less than lady-like. On the one hand, we socialize boys and men with the violence that creates the need for a body farm, but on the other hand, of course it's women cleaning up the messes, unafraid to look at the product of that violence and be honest about what it means.

How much revision went into this poem?

This poem was almost twice the length in its first version (and it's still a lengthy poem). I realized a few drafts in that I didn't want to focus on describing the dead bodies as much as the living women studying them. Once I had that focus, there was a shift and about half the poem fell away so I could highlight those characters instead.

What is your favorite line from the poem or the line you are most proud of?

"getting dark purge fluid on her coat sleeves," is definitely my favorite line. I just couldn't get the phrase purge fluid out of my head when I heard it described in the podcast that triggered this poem. What a bizarrely technical but also totally gross name. It felt like the exact balance I was going for when describing these scientists studying death.

How long have you been writing poetry? What has changed from your first poem to your newest?

I've been writing since I was a little kid. From when I started thinking about poetry as a regular artistic pursuit—maybe in high school—until now, the biggest way I've grown is a simultaneous clarity of vision while trying to hold that vision at arm's length. I have a much better idea of what I want to say in my work, but also as I learn to see that more clearly, I want to describe it more obliquely.

Who are some of your favorite poets?

Muriel Rukeyser will always be one of my favorites. She was a queer Jewish poet who was completely unafraid to break the rules of poetry at the time. Her poetry on the page looks like something from today's magazines, and she's got a balance of human political attention and surrealism that I'll always be envious of. Adrienne Rich is another queer Jewish poet I read over and over again. I could read her *Twenty-One Love Poems* every day and find something new.

Do you work in any other artistic mediums? If so, how do those other genres inform your poetry?

I play guitar and sing, and I'm working hard on mandolin. One of my ongoing projects is writing new tunes to old Jewish texts, psalms, and prayers. The words exist, but the rhythms and harmonies can make them feel and mean something different. I think this is a helpful parallel for a poem like this one. I had a story and a text I was working from. My job as a poet was to take the story and make new music for it. You can read an essay about body farms, then this poem, and hopefully they'll feel like two different tunes for the same words.

Based on your personal experience, what advice would you give to other writers?

The advice I give is often most difficult for me to follow: avoid too much messaging, especially when beginning a poem. I am someone with something to say about what it means to be Jewish, to be queer, to be mixed-race, but if I start a poem with that message it always becomes pedantic. Instead, I start with images or with word play. This poem is a perfect example. I definitely had something to say about femininity, but it comes through better as "it takes both hands / to brush off the maggots" instead of "women and femmes will get messy with death because we're already closest to it."

What drew you to *Driftwood Press*?

I saw a lot of body parts in the poems y'all have published, and so I hoped this poem would fit in. So much of my poetry is stuck in my body, and sometimes it needs to push out violently. Y'all seemed open to that feeling. Also, the author interviews are cool, especially for a poet with only a handful of magazine credits like me.

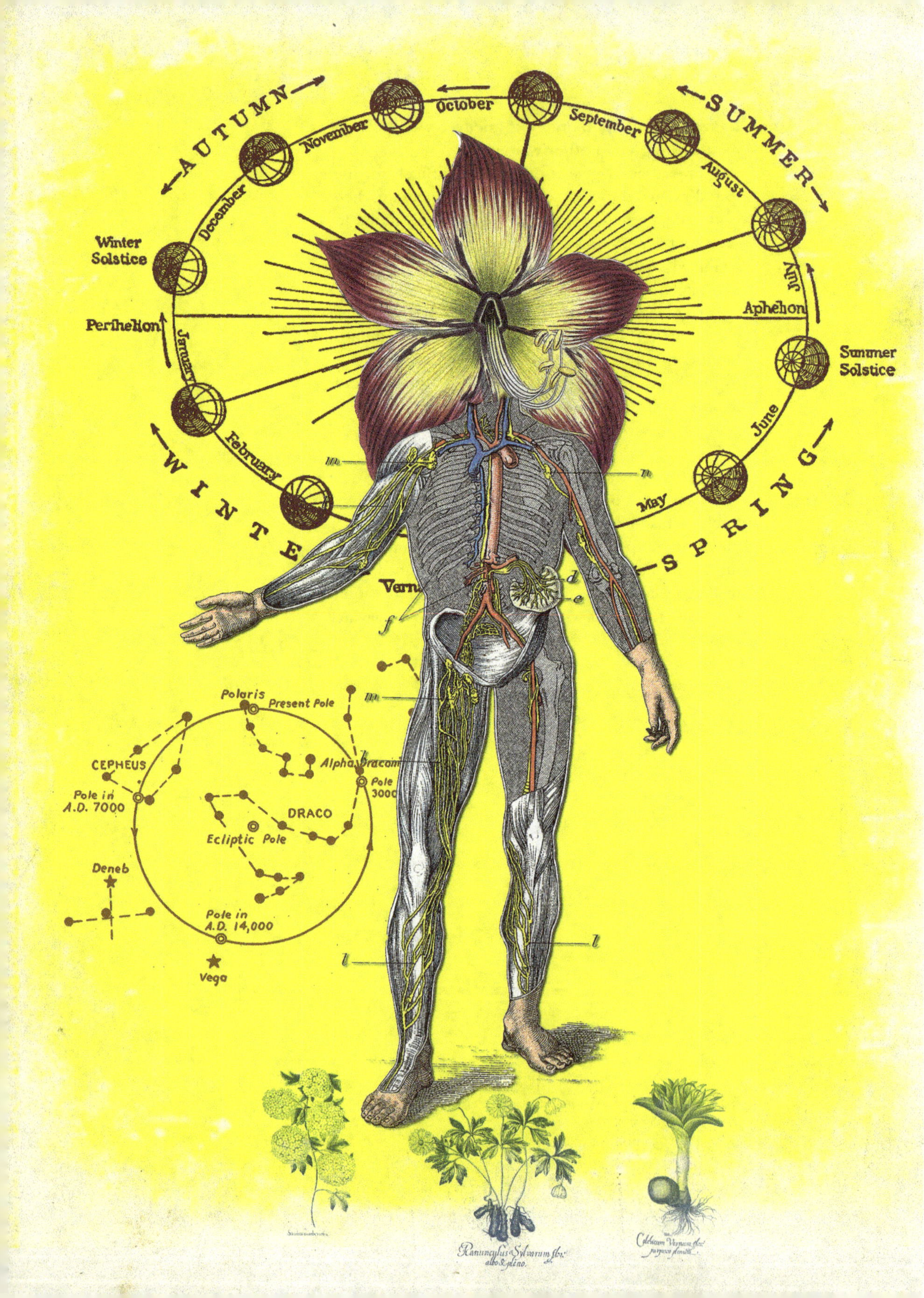

"LYMPHATIC MAN" | THOMAS TERCEIRA

HA HA HA HAHA

HA LAUGH TRACK HA

HA HA HA HA HA

BY:

J. COLLINGS

HA HA HA HA HA HA HA HA HA
HA HA HA HA HA HA HA HA
HA HA HA HA HA HA HA HA
HA HA HA HA HA HA HA
HA HA HA HA HA

HA HA HA HA HA HA HA HA HA HA HA HA HA HA HA HA HA HA HA HA HA HA HA HA HA HA HA HA HA HA HA HA HA

HA HA HA HA HA

HA HA HA HA HA
HA HA
HA HA
HA HA
HA HA
HA HA
HA HA
HA HA
HA HA
HA HA
HA HA
HA HA
HA HA
HA HA HA HA HA
HA HA HA HA HA HA HA HA HA HA HA HA HA

HA HA HA HA HA HA HA HA HA HA HA HA

HA HA HA HA HA HA HA HA HA HA HA HA HA HA HA

HA HA HA HA HA HA HA HA HA HA HA HA HA HA

HA HA HA HA HA HA HA HA HA

HA HA HA

HA HA HA HA HA HA HA HA

HA HA HA HA HA HA HA HA HA HA HA HA HA HA

HA HA HA

AH AH

HA HA HA

HA HA HA HA HA HA HA HA HA HA HA HA HA HA HA

HA HA HA HA HA HA HA HA HA HA HA HA

OPEN MIC NIGHT

HA HA HA

HA HA HA HA HA

HA HA HA

HA HA HA HA HA HA HA

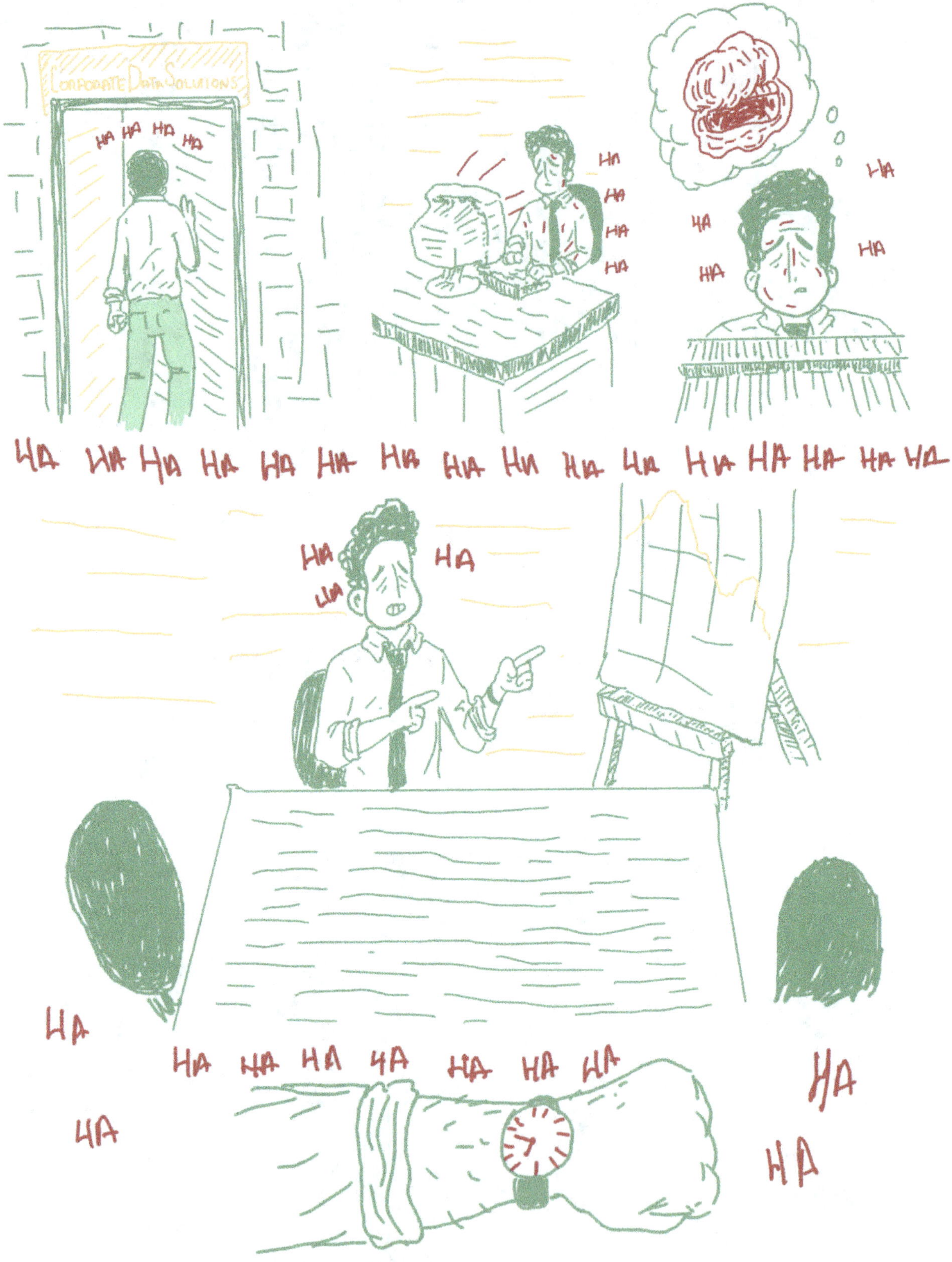

HA HA HA HA HA HA HA HA HA HA HA HA HA HA HA HA

HA HA HA HA

HA

HA HA HA HA HA HA HA

HA

HA

HA

CORPORATE DATA SOLUTIONS
OPEN MIC NIGHT
OPEN MIC
SIGN UP

HA HA HA HA HA HA H-
HA
HA

Interview

J. Collings

What inspired "LaughTrack"?

Before I started working on LaughTrack, I filled a sketchbook with drawings of the main character. I envisioned him as a total sad-sack who could barely function in the real world. A lot of times I just had him echo some of my nonsense anxieties, and when I drew him sad about the same things I was sad about, somehow I was able to remove myself from my own problems and start to laugh at them.

Is any aspect of "LaughTrack" autobiographical? Have you ever dabbled in live comedy?

The only time I came close was when I took an english elective about stand-up comedy in college. I'm pretty sure its the only time they offered the class, but the teacher was a fiction writer with a passion for analyzing stand-up, and he offered a choice for the final exam: write an essay or do a stand-up set for the class. I chose to do a set, and I still want to cringe into myself whenever I think about it.

What's autobiographical isn't the stand-up portion though, it's the fight within yourself to try something creative and failing. Thinking you have potential and failing hard is something I think a lot of artists can associate with.

Aside from the recurring laughs, "LaughTrack" is a wordless comic. What are the benefits of having a comic told almost solely through visual imagery? What are the challenges?

I had a poetry teacher that used to say, "End on an image and don't explain it." He argued that there is something wonderful about audiences assigning meaning to images, especially ones that defy their attempts. When I'm writing something silent, it's easy to worry that my point can't come through without language, but I love it when the images are evocative enough for the audience to prescribe their own meanings. And the meanings the audience create for themselves are often much more interesting than what the author intended. I remember after I saw *2001: A Space Odyssey*, I was floored by the oddness of the final scenes, but after I heard Kubrick explain how it's a kind of human zoo, I was disappointed and bored.

Could you talk about your use of colors in this piece? How did you decide which colors to use when?

I saw the colors as a subtle way to develop a wordless language for the comic. I stole the idea from David Mazzucchelli's graphic novel *Asterios Polyp*, which is one of my favorites. After I read it, I became obsessive with the color palette and the way it shifted between scenes, moods, and characters. I love the idea of mapping meaning to colors, and the way it can make a reader feel like a conspiracy theorist by searching for meaning in every corner of the work.

What are some of your biggest comic inspirations?

Calvin and Hobbes by Bill Watterson (I read this as much as I could as a kid); *Blankets* by Craig Thompson (I made so many friends read this in high school); *Jimmy Corrigan* and *Building Stories* by Chris Ware; *How to Be Happy* by Eleanor Davis; *Asterios Polyp* by David Mazzucchelli; *Very Casual* by Michael DeForge; *Megg and Mogg* comics by Simon Hanselmann; *Understanding Comics* by Scott McCloud; *Killing and Dying* and *Shortcomings* by Adrian Tomine; *Boundless* by Jillian Tamaki.

I have to stop, or this list will get out of hand.

THE SALTON SEA

BY CINDY HOUSE

THE TEACHER FOR YOUR GIFTED PROGRAM CALLS ONE NIGHT DURING THE SECOND TO LAST WEEK OF FOURTH GRADE. YOU REFUSE TO DO THE FINAL MAPPING PROJECT FOR THE GEOGRAPHY UNIT, SHE SAYS.

I SAY I THINK YOU HAVE DYSCALCULIA, A MATH LEARNING DISABILITY. ENLARGING A MAP WITH A GRID SYSTEM, WITH ALL THOSE CALCULATIONS, IS EXACTLY THE KIND OF THING THAT IS AFFECTED BY DYSCALCULIA.

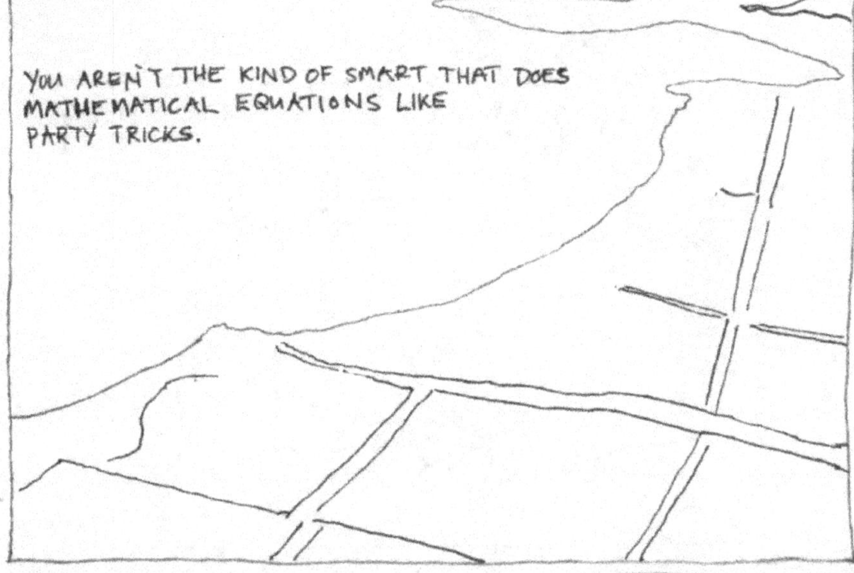

I SAY YOU ARE A POET, THAT YOU JUST PUBLISHED A POEM. YOU ARE A TEN-YEAR-OLD POET. SHE SAYS YOU NEVER TOLD HER THAT.

"CAN HE WRITE A POEM ABOUT A PLACE FOR HIS FINAL PROJECT?" SHE ASKS. "SOMETHING LIKE A TRAVEL BROCHURE. MAKE US WANT TO GO THERE. SELL IT."

YOUR POEMS DO NOT REALLY SELL THINGS.

MOTEL

YOU'VE BEEN OBSESSED
WITH THE HOLOCAUST SINCE
YOU WERE SIX-YEARS-OLD.
YOU TITLED YOUR
LAST POEM "THE MOON
SMELLS LIKE GUNPOWDER."

SO I GIVE YOU THE SALTON SEA.

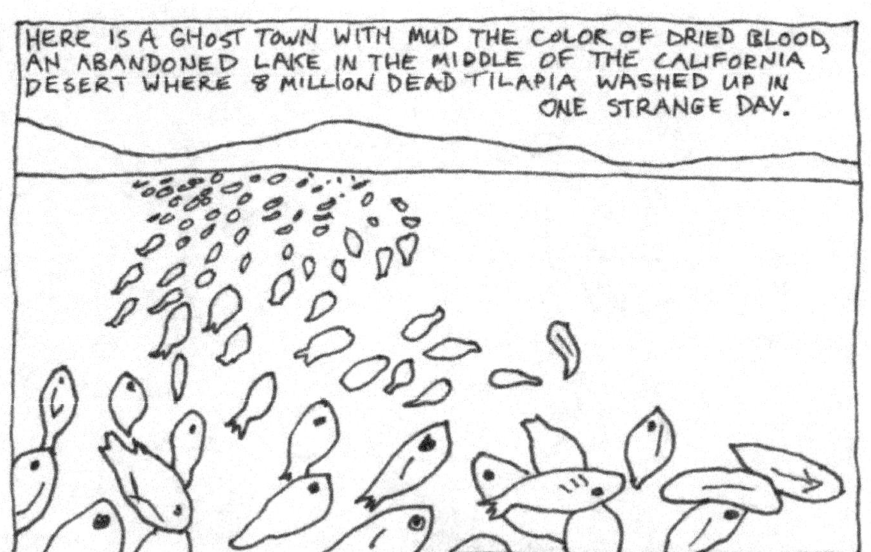
HERE IS A GHOST TOWN WITH MUD THE COLOR OF DRIED BLOOD, AN ABANDONED LAKE IN THE MIDDLE OF THE CALIFORNIA DESERT WHERE 8 MILLION DEAD TILAPIA WASHED UP IN ONE STRANGE DAY.

THIS IS A PLACE WITH DIRT CLOUDS THICK ENOUGH TO BLUR THE OTHER SIDE OF THE STREET AND MOST PEOPLE HAVE INHALERS AND NEBULIZERS BECAUSE THE DUST FROM THE DEAD AND DYING LAKE IS CHOKING AND CAKING THEIR LUNGS.

I GIVE YOU THE
LIKE GREEN
SALTON SEA, WITH IT'S ALGAE POOLS
CROP CIRCLES, VISIBLE FOR MILES.

ABANDONED FURNITURE, RIPPED AND DISCARDED ON THE SAND. IF YOU SQUINT, YOU CAN ALMOST PRETEND THE OWNERS WILL BE RIGHT BACK TO SIT DOWN ONCE THE COMMERCIAL IS OVER AND THE POPCORN IS POPPED.

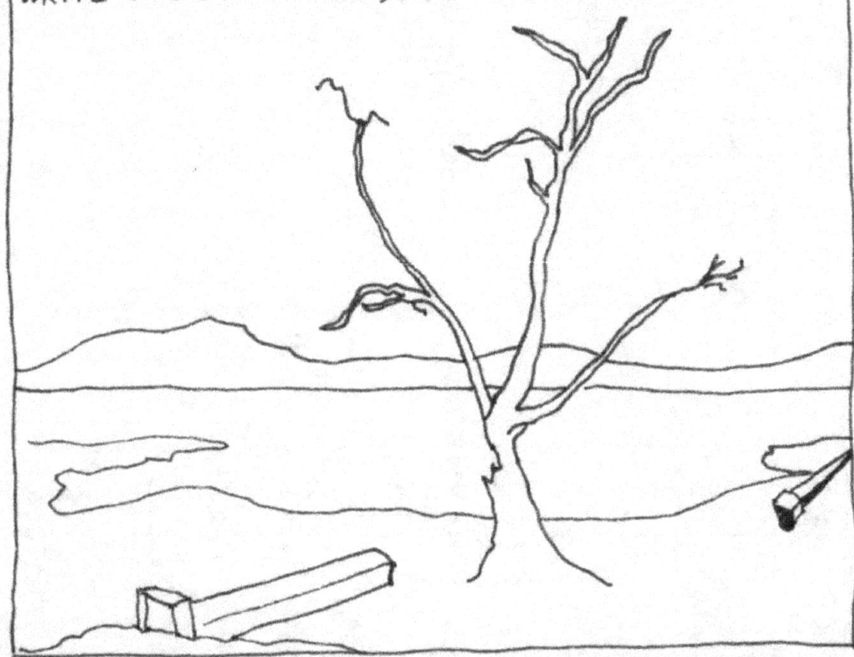
I WANT TO GIFT YOU WITH THE LESSON OF HOW TO MAKE AN ILL-SUITED EDUCATION WORK FOR YOU. DON'T DRAW THE PALM TREES AND THE UMBRELLA DRINKS. DON'T WRITE THE BROCHURE. DON'T DO AS YOU'RE TOLD.

SEE THE DEAD FISH, THE TOXIC AIR. SEE THE MOTOR BOATS ROTTING ON PULVERIZED FISH BONES LIKE WHALE CORPSES. THIS IS GEOGRAPHY YOU CAN WRITE ABOUT.

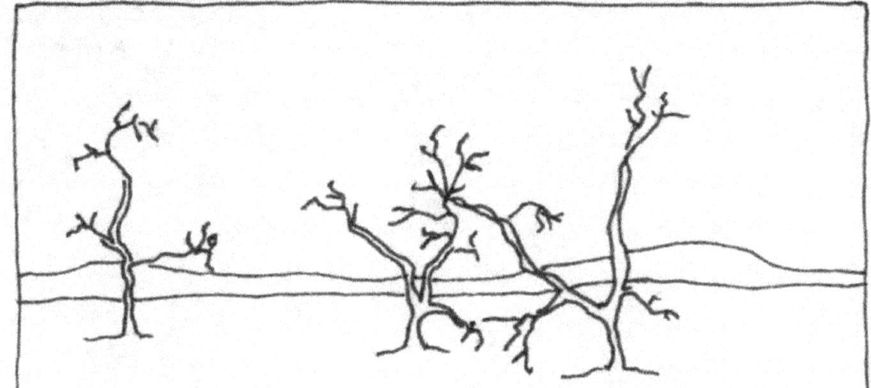
YOU ALREADY LIKE TO LIFT UP THE CORNERS OF LIFE AND SEE WHAT DARK THING IS GROWING UNDERNEATH. THIS IS YOUR KIND OF LANDSCAPE.

THE SALTON SEA IS YOUR POEM READY TO BE WRITTEN FROM THE FIRST GOOGLE IMAGE YOU PULL UP, THE FIRST LINE YOU READ ABOUT HOW THIS HAPPENED AND WHY.
HOPE HAS LEFT
THE WORDS WILL DROP INTO PLACE, MAPPING THEMSELVES OUT INSIDE OF YOU.

Interview

CINDY HOUSE

Is any aspect of "The Salton Sea" autobiographical?

It's completely autobiographical.

I have an amazing eleven-year-old son and this piece came from being a witness to how he learns and what grabs him and won't let go. Last year, after masking it for most of his elementary school career thus far, I realized that he probably had a math learning disability, which he has since been diagnosed with. He's in the gifted program at school so he's very smart, but this struggle with certain things came to a head. And it was the end of the year and he was just done. His teacher called me because he had refused to do his final project, which wasn't like him. When she offered an alternative project, I just could have wept with gratitude for her willingness to *see* him. That day, I happened to read this fascinating article about a dying lake in the California dessert that had once been a fashionable resort area and I knew that if my son had to write a poem about a location, this was a place he could fall inside and get lost in for a while. He has obsessions with disasters, with the worst periods in history, with people and places that are dark and ruined and sad. He won't read Harry Potter, but he has a collection of Middle Grade and Young Adult novels about the Holocaust that is pretty extensive.

What inspired "The Salton Sea"?

The idea that, for me, being a parent at times is like being a curator for someone new to everything, someone you love more than anyone in the world. I remember when he was a newborn, looking into his face and thinking, you've never seen the ocean or *The Wizard of Oz* or a Blue Jay. You haven't heard what a violin sounds like and you don't know what a pomegranate is. You don't know Flanney O'Connor or Basquiat or Beethoven. And I am the one who will be choosing what to show you.

And the piece is also about how to help a very bright child learn to navigate a system that is not ideal, that is not serving his soul. I want him to learn to work and to tolerate boredom without losing his fascination and wonder at this world we live in.

For readers who don't know, can you fill us in a little on what the Salton Sea is?

It's this incredible place in the desert of California that is like a wasteland but once was a popular resort destination in the seventies. It's a giant lake that is dying. Over the years, the increased salinity and pollution from agricultural runoff caused a stench that basically turned it into a ghost town. Now it is nothing but abandoned motels, dead fish washed up on the sand, and algae blooms.

Our editors would classify this work as a poem-comic. Do you think that's an accurate classification? What does it mean to be a poem-comic?

I happen to know some incredible poets and I'm afraid to put the word poem near anything I make because it feels like the one thing I cannot write. Nothing would paralyze me faster while working than being called any kind of poet. This is the curse of knowing wildly talented poets before I've ever tried to write poetry, maybe.

But having said that, I will just add that I like the term because it opens up the idea of what comics or graphic narrative work can be. "Comics" feels so narrow and when I think of a book like *My Favorite Thing is Monsters* by Emil Ferris or *Persepolis* by Marjane Satrapi, "comics" just isn't quite right.

And I will also say that I mostly write short stories and essays, but I went to the School of the Art Institute of Chicago for my undergrad. I just didn't make visual art of any kind for the last couple of decades. But when I have an idea about my son, I need imagery. I need to draw pictures. It's as if words aren't quite enough. Poem-comic feels like a term that needs to exist because there are pieces that tell a story that isn't linear, a story that is really a feeling or a moment.

How did "The Salton Sea" change from its first draft?

The first draft of "The Salton Sea" was closer to an essay. But I knew I would add drawings and I knew it wouldn't work as an essay, so I was just trying to get the feeling down. And then I had to chip away at it and cut almost all of it to get to just the essence of that very specific feeling I had that made me want to write it. And I don't usually work that way. I don't write more than I know I will need. Once I started the drawings, I was able to see more clearly what needed to stay and what could go.

The comic seems to be drawn on pieces of small paper—they almost look like napkins. Then they seem to have been photographed, rather than scanned. Could you talk a little about what this methodology adds to the texture of the work?

I work on watercolor blocks of paper and I love Strathmore 5.5 by 8.5 blocks so much that I periodically stock up just in case they stop making them. I have a really solid stash right now. The paper is thick and textured to hold water, but I like the way it feels under my pen. The pages are actually scanned, but I think because the paper is smaller than the screen and I don't crop them, they end up looking photographed. I like the way they look like found sketches, like they aren't fussed over or cherished.

Handwritten lettering is used in many of our favorite comics and graphic novels. What do you think it adds to the reading experience?

I think when the story is intimate and personal, it makes it feel like something closer to a journal entry. I don't have the same distance with my graphic work as I do with stories and even essays that I write. And I like having the feeling as a reader that I am reading something private, something written in the author's own handwriting. It makes me think of being in art school when everyone had a black, hard cover sketch book and I could swap books with a friend and look at all of her sketches and notes and plans for projects.

Who/what are some of your biggest comic inspirations?

David Smalls' book *Stitches* gutted me. I just love everything about that book. The story, the gray scale drawings, the variety in the panels. What a beautiful use of the medium of graphic narrative. It still kills me just thinking about it. I also loved *Fun House.* I think it's brilliant the way she inserted drawings of real photos and changed her style for those drawings—the way they are more realistic and less comic-y. I can't say enough about how smart I think that choice was. And I stumbled upon an anthology of graphic narrative short pieces all dealing with the Las Vegas shooting a year ago, a book called *Where We Live: A Benefit for the Survivors in Las Vegas.* I thought it was amazing to see such a huge selection of writers and artists all taking on the same tragic event. Each piece was so different, and it was a way of swimming in every angle imaginable of what happened that night. Some of the work was so startling and emotional. It really stretched my way of thinking about comics and opened it wider for me.

What other mediums have influenced your work? How?

Photography—I love to look at a photo and think about all the storylines in the image. I have a photo in my house that a friend gave me—she's a photo journalist and a fine art photographer. It's been on my wall for close to a year, and I still stop and stand in front of it and think about it in new ways. It's a picture of a row of people watching the eclipse from the summer before last. I think about the way their clothes tell me things about them, the lack of sturdiness in their lawn chairs, the way they are sitting. There is so much information, so many ways to daydream my own stories from that one second when the lens caught them. It helps me to remember to try to make careful choices in my own work.

Where can our readers find more of your work? Have you been published before?

I have essays published at *Literary Mama, The Rumpus*, and *So To Speak*. And I have a short story at *The Drum: A Literary Magazine for Your Ears,* with more work coming out soon at *Longleaf Review, Wigleaf,* and the *Lily Poetry Review.*

For any of our readers who are aspiring artists, what is one piece of advice you wished someone would have told you when you started drawing comics?

Pick supplies you can carry with you so you can work anywhere. I was at Beavertail Island in Jamestown, RI last summer, and the wind was blowing my hair in my face, and I could hardly see as the sun was going down, but I sat on the rocks and just made sketches for panels. I drew my son parcouring over the rocks and then lying flat on his back like a starfish, and I drew the waves and the lighthouse. And I don't know if I'll use those panels for anything but the practice is invaluable, the way it trains me to panel up the world around me, to frame my ideas in that way.

What are you working on now?

I have a few things I'm working on. I have an essay collection that needs maybe three more pieces before it's complete. With the current news cycle, every day, I think, I should write an essay about that. I also have a short story collection that is almost complete. And I'm halfway through a graphic novel about co-parenting with a narcissist. If I could stop sleeping so I could get all of my ideas down, I would be thrilled.

What drew you to *Driftwood Press*?

I love *Driftwood Press* so much. It's one of my favorite magazines. There is great variety in the work, but being safe is not one of your aims. I feel like I could find anything in *Driftwood Press* and it would not surprise me, but the one consistent thing is that the work is quality work. I think of a story like "A Fresh Dog," and I am thrilled all over again to be published at *Driftwood.* That story shook me up. I'm still shook just thinking about it. It's the kind of story where the walls of your house could be coming down around you and you'd say, "I just have to finish this paragraph."

I WATCHED HIM CREATE FOR YEARS.

LONG BEFORE THE CONSERVANCY EVER CAUGHT WIND OF HIS TALENT, HE TURNED OUR NEIGHBORHOOD INTO A LIVING MENAGERIE.

TO GROW UP IMMERSED IN A WORLD OF EXOTIC POSSIBILITIES LEFT AN INDELLIBLE MARK UPON ME. TO WATCH A MAN CREATE, EVEN WHEN NO ONE ASKED HIM TO.

THEN THE ARTICLES. THE INTERVIEWS, THE PHOTO SHOOTS.
THE PRESTIGIOUS INVITATION FROM THE CONSERVANCY TO CREATE
SOMETHING ON A GRAND AND NATIONAL SCALE.

IT WAS MORE THAN RECOGNITION. HIS EXHIBITION, WITH ITS CAROUSEL CENTERPIECE, WAS AN OPPORTUNITY TO SHARE WITH THE WORLD— AND ALLOW OTHERS TO INTERACT WITH HIS.

IT WAS THE CULMINATION OF A JOURNEY.

ONE THAT WAS BOTH BEAUTIFUL... AND FLEETING.

NO ONE HAD THOUGHT ABOUT THE STRESS TO THE PLANTS.
THE WEIGHT OF ALL THOSE BODIES. THEIR REVOLUTIONS.
I FELT THE LOSS MUST SURELY WITHER HIM TOO... BUT IT DID NOT.

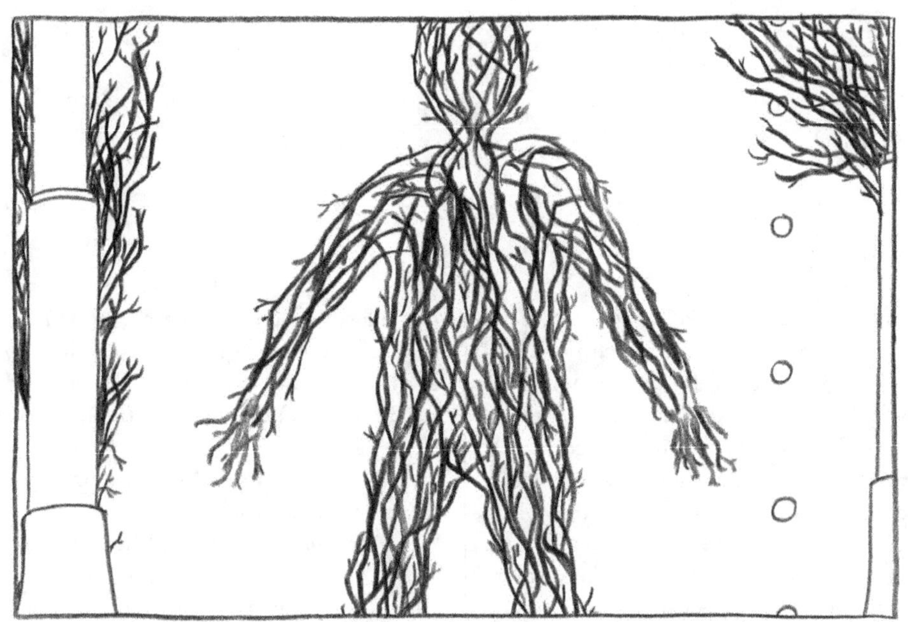

HE ONCE TOLD ME, "TO UNDERSTAND THE IMMIGRANT EXPERIENCE, YOU HAVE TO LOOK DEEPER THAN THE ACCENTS, THE PATTERNED CLOTHES, THE FOODS, THE RITUAL TRADITIONS. EVEN OUR STORIES."

INTERVIEW

JASON HART

What inspired "Émigré Animals"?

My mother is a first-generation, Czech-born immigrant, so a lot of my childhood identity is wrapped up in the pride and perspective that she and my grandparents had for both America and our heritage. Czech folktales, soups, polkas, stories of Christmas carps and escaping Communism all fill my early memories. I've done allegories for their experience in older stories, but with immigrant and nationalist issues filling America's consciousness last year, I began to think about what it means to be a first generation born in America today. There is pride, but there's also an anchorlessness. I've visited the thirteenth century castle in my mother's hometown, but I can't speak the language. In the flight toward freedom, our parents gave up the deep foundation of their surroundings, and "Émigré Animals" was born out of that.

Our editors would classify this work as a poem-comic. Do you think that's an accurate classification? What does it mean to be a poem-comic?

I can understand that classification. Poetry comics, being a hybrid medium, exists across such a wide spectrum that I think the form may be as much defined by the reader's interpretation and experience as by the structure itself. I hadn't thought of "Émigré Animals" as a poem-comic because of the emphasis I'd put on the narrative, but from a different perspective, yes, I think it can fit there.

How did "Émigré Animals" change from its first draft?

"Émigré Animals" first began as a poem (so I guess I lose the previous argument). After jotting out the core idea, I fumbled my control over some disparate allusions and streams of thought. In reigning it back in, the image of a carousel with topiary animals crystalized—and not knowing exactly what it meant yet, I could feel that this was the spine of the piece.

Tell us a little more about the process of drafting "Émigré Animals."

I struggled with a few different drafts before simplifying it down to its published form. Early on, I still clung to the original poem, which contained some of those warring allusions and addressed my mother directly. As the text became more narration-driven, I explored a few eccentric dead ends. In one, the character who later evolved into the invisible narrator was first a sort of spectral child. In another, the topiarist was an anthropomorphic elephant. It took a while to realize that straight-forward was the right approach.

Is any aspect of "Émigré Animals" autobiographical?

Not directly, although the piece is wrapped around my memories of my grandfather, both the kind of man he was and the emotions of spending time with him.

What was the hardest part of crafting "Émigré Animals"?

With short comics, I usually have a clear idea of the work from early on. There's a relationship between the words and images, the structure, style, and theme that locks together so that I can see the main point-of-impact. When a piece evolves as this one did, unsuccessful ideas can linger and crowd out that synergy. It's more of a struggle to trim it down to the necessities. Even after completion, it takes longer to be able to evaluate objectively.

Can you talk about your decision to mostly stick to two panels per page? Craft-wise, what effect does this paneling produce?

It was more instinct than deliberate choice, but I think I wanted to play with essentially a three-panel structure, where the middle panel is a dissociated voice. I love the rhythm of three-panel comics, and by paring it down to two (with the voice in the gutter), it slows the reader down and gives each image greater significance. The more structured a comic, the more it evokes a traditional or literary sense, which I also wanted for this story.

Handwritten lettering is used in many of our favorite comics and graphic novels. What do you think it adds to the reading experience?

A fellow cartoonist beat into me the importance of hand lettering wherever possible. Especially when moving away from the traditional aesthetic of inked artwork, it's essential that the lettering feels cohesive with the art, and it's really difficult to achieve that with digital fonts and balloons. Beyond that, it's also a very personal connection with the author—the character of their handwriting.

Our editors were unanimously impressed with this comic's ability to—in such a short space—be emotional, nuanced, original, and effective. Could you delve a little into what makes a short comic work?

It really is about finding, if possible, that moment where the visuals and the writing strike against each other in an impactful way—and then making the rest of the story serve that climax succinctly. It's a fine dance between brevity and the elements that create tone, pacing, emotion, and style. Plus, lots of ruthless editing.

What instruments did you use to craft "Émigré Animals"?

First, pages and pages of notes and dialogue, followed by one-inch thumbnails, went into a pocket notebook. Next, the panel outlines and lettering guides were laid out on the computer, then printed at actual size. I drew pencil underdrawings directly onto these sheets and enlarged them from 8.5" x 11" to 11" x 17". These "penciled pages" went onto a light box, where I created the final artwork (panel art, borders, and hand lettering) using black colored pencil on Bristol board. The pages were scanned back in, touched up on the computer, and collated into the final comic.

Who/what are some of your biggest comic inspirations?

I'll never fully shake Paul Pope from my style. He was the first comic cartoonist I idolized. Eleanor Davis, Jordi LaFebre, Gabriel Bá, Kerascöet, Antoine Cossé, Guy Davis, Romuald Reutimann, Sammy Harkham, and Rubén Pellejero have filled in some of the blanks of the storyteller I'd like to be.

What other mediums have influenced your work? How?

TV and movies, fashion, children's books, design—anything that is a vehicle for visual storytelling. I gain the most inspiration, though, from prose—classic Russian literature (Tolstoy, Dostoevsky, Lermontov) and American short stories and novels (Paul Bowles, Quan Barry, Karen Russell, Steinbeck, Hemmingway).

Where can our readers find more of your work? Have you been published before?

Most of my online activity is through Instagram (@json.hart) and Facebook (/jasonhart.comics). The Facebook page has a list of my published works, but a few journals I've been in recently include *Illustoria, Geometry, Ink Brick, New Plains Review*, and *Barrelhouse*.

For any of our readers who are aspiring artists, what is one piece of advice you wished someone would have told you when you started drawing comics?

Write, lay out, and draw with the spread in consideration. Printed comics exist as two visible pages, not one. Use that to its fullest potential, and be conscious of the power of the page-turn.

What are you working on now?

The comic on my drawing table now is called "Lonely Satellite." After a few more, I'd like to publish a collection of my short comics from the past few years. I've also got some prose short stories I'm writing. And as always, working on being a decent father, husband, and neighbor.

What drew you to *Driftwood Press*?

I'd first seen *Driftwood Press* on NewPages and even submitted a comic a while ago. But the recent push for more comics material and the new graphic novel open-call made me take a look at the publication anew. The cover illustrations, clean design, and comics entries of the last few issues made it very appealing.

Is there anything else you'd like to tell us about this work in particular?

The first lines of the original "Émigré Animals" poem were, "Mother, you could not know what it means to be born here / Beneath this lamp light of a thousand suns / Each shining from its own distant seat in the universe…" And there were no anthropomorphic elephants in it either.

CONTRIBUTORS

CLAIRE AGNES is a writer originally from West Chester, Pennsylvania. She was the recipient of the 2015 Rowan Award for Women Writers in Fiction and her creative nonfiction has been published in *Entropy*. She has received residency at Stone Court and was a Global Research Fellow in Prague. She is a curator for the KGB Emerging Writers Reading Series and an assistant fiction editor for the *Washington Square Review*. She currently lives in Brooklyn, where she is a cat mom, MFA candidate, and professor at New York University.

SHANE PAGE is a graduate student at Missouri State University. His work has appeared in *The Molotov Cocktail, Pank, Hobart,* and *Occulum.*

JULIA B. LEVINE has won numerous awards for her work, including the 2015 Northern California Book Award in Poetry for her latest collection, *Small Disasters Seen in Sunlight* (*LSU Press,* 2014), which inaugurated the Barataria Poetry Series; the 2003 Tampa Review Poetry Prize for *Ask*; and the 1998 Anhinga Poetry prize as well as a bronze medal from *Foreword Magazine* for her first collection, *Practicing for Heaven.* She lives and works in Davis, California.

ROY WHITE is a blind person who lives in Saint Paul, Minnesota with a lovely human and an affable lab mix. His work has appeared or is forthcoming in *Poetry Magazine, BOAAT Journal, Kenyon Review, Copper Nickel,* and elsewhere. He can be found on Twitter (@ surrealroy).

CRYSTAL STONE's poetry has previously appeared or is forthcoming in *Occulum, Anomaly, BONED, Eunoia Review, isacoustics, Tuck Magazine, Writers Resist, Drunk Monkeys, Coldnoon, Poets Reading the News, Jet Fuel Review, Sigma Tau Delta Rectangle, North Central Review, Badlands Review, Green Blotter, Southword Journal Online,* and *Dylan Days.* She is currently pursuing her MFA at Iowa State University, she's given a TEDx talk on poetry, and her first collection of poetry, *Knock-Off Monarch*, is forthcoming from *Dawn Valley Press* this autumn. You can find her on Twitter (@justlikeastone8) and on instagram (@stone.flowering).

ZACHARY ELLER lives in Jersey City, New Jersey. His work has previously appeared in *Cha: An Asian Literary Journal, Ghost City Review,* and *Waxing & Waning.*

ANNETTE SCHLICHTER lives and writes in Southern California. A former professor of Comparative Literature (University of California Irvine), she published a range of academic pieces in German and English. Since 2012, she has been writing poetry in En glish. Her work has appeared in a couple of journals, and in the summer of 2017, *ghost city press* published her micro chapbook, *Like Love.*

JOSHUA SILAVENT is an award-winning journalist based in the greater Atlanta area. He was named Beat Reporter of the Year in Georgia by the *Associated Press* in 2015 for his extensive reporting on homelessness and affordable housing shortages. Silavent's first and lasting love is writing lyrical and narrative poetry.

JACQUELINE BERGER's fourth book, *The Day You Miss Your Exit,* was published by *Broadstone Books* in 2018. Her previous books include *The Gift That Arrives*

Broken, winner of the 2010 Autumn House Poetry Prize, and *Things That Burn*, selected by Mark Strand as the 2004 winner of the Agha Shahid Ali Prize. Her poetry has been featured on Garrison Keillor's Writers Almanac. Individual poems have been published in numerous anthologies and journals, including *The Iowa Review, American Poetry: The Next Generation, On The Verge, Old Dominion Review, Rhino, River Styx,* and *Nimrod.* She directs the Master of Arts in English program at Notre Dame de Namur University in Belmont, California and lives in San Francisco.

TARA ROEDER is the author of the chapbooks *(all the things you're not)* and *Maritime*. Her work has appeared in venues including *3:AM Magazine, THRUSH, The Bombay Gin,* and *Hobart.* Her most recent project is the *DIAGRAM Press* chapbook *Every Bird Is A Miracle*, a collaboration with visual artist Arman Safa. She is an Associate Professor of Writing in Queens, New York.

RAINIE OET is a nonbinary writer, poetry editor at Salt Hill, and the author of *No Mark Spiral* (*CutBank Books*, 2018). Their work appears in *The Yale Review, jubilat, The Adroit Journal, Colorado Review,* and *Poetry Review*, among other publications. They won the inaugural *Press 53* Flash Fiction Contest in 2018. They are an MFA candidate in Poetry at Syracuse University, where they were awarded the Shirley Jackson Prize in Fiction. You can read more on their website (rainieoet.com).

MARY MAROSTE received her BA in Creative Writing from Western Michigan University, and is pursuing an MFA at Virginia Commonwealth. She is the recipient of the AWP Intro Journals Project for her poem "Landscape with Sharp Rocks." Her work has been featured or is forthcoming in *Mid-American Review, Jabberwock Review, Pittsburgh Poetry Review,* and *Winter Tangerine.* Her chapbook, *Blueprint for a Home Without Tampons,* was published by *dancing girl press.* She is from Houghton, Michigan but currently resides and studies in Richmond.

JOSHUA SASSOON OROL is a trans Jewish poet from Raleigh, NC, writing with the texts, tunes, and stories passed down from their mixed heritage family. Joshua completed an MFA at NC State University and received an Academy of American Poets prize while at UNC Chapel Hill. Their work has most recently been published in the *Jewish Literary Journal, Nimrod,* and the *Mizmor 2018 Anthology of Jewish Poetry.*

ALEXANDER LANDERMAN is currently working as a freelance artist spending his summer traveling across the United States as a resident artist.

THOMAS TERCEIRA collects old photos, images, and illustrations from old and forgotten books and vintage ephemera. He started making collages with these materials and has found it both rewarding and challenging.

J. COLLINGS went to school for English and Creative Writing. He teaches kids how to write arguments and read books. He lives in Ohio with a pretty cool cat.

CINDY HOUSE has an MFA from Lesley University and lives in New Haven, CT with her husband and her eleven-year-old son. She is a 2018 recipient of an emerging artist grant from the St. Botolph Club Foundation, and she opened for David Sedaris in two cities in April of this year. She has published or has work forthcoming at *The Drum: A Literary Magazine for Your Ears, The Rumpus, So To Speak, The Lily Poetry Review,* and *Longleaf Review.*

JASON HART is a visual storyteller based in Dayton, Ohio. He works by day as an advertising art director, crafting brands' stories—and all night as a comics cartoonist, creating narratives of his own. His most recent works appear in *Illustoria, Barrelhouse, Ink Brick, UPPERCASE, New Plains Review, Geometry, Flock*, and elsewhere.

www.ingramcontent.com/pod-product-compliance
Lightning Source LLC
Chambersburg PA
CBHW082123180726
48291CB00011B/2820

* 9 7 8 1 9 4 9 0 6 5 0 1 5 *